STRANGE But True
Baseball Stories

STRANGE
But True
Baseball Stories

by Furman Bisher

ILLUSTRATED WITH PHOTOGRAPHS

RANDOM HOUSE · NEW YORK

This title was originally catalogued by the Library of Congress as follows:

Bisher, Furman.
   Strange but true baseball stories. New York, Random House ₍1966₎

   186 p. ports. 24 cm. (Little League library, 4)

   1. Baseball stories—Juvenile literature.   I. Title.

GV873.B5   796.3570922   65–10492

Library of Congress   ₍8₎

Photograph Credits: Odell Barbary, page 32; Furman Bisher, pages 45, 88; Culver Pictures, pages 79, 92, 127, 128, 149, 160; The *News*, page 182; Sy Seidman, page 162; United Press International, pages 10, 12, 60, 72, 74, 104, 108, 116, 137, 141, 143, 169; Wide World, pages 4, 7, 20, 36, 40, 53, 55, 62, 67, 80, 100, 113, 119, 135, 146, 166, 181.

Cover art by Tom Beecham

Manufactured in the United States of America

Designed by Jackie Corner

Trade Ed.: ISBN: 0-394-80184-9   Lib. Ed.: ISBN: 0-394-90184-3

CONTENTS

INTRODUCTION

There is a popular misconception that baseball is a game played nine men to the side. This is for narrow people, those who believe that horseshoes can be played only by horses.

Baseball can be played by any number from two on up. It can be played late at night, early in the morning, in the middle of the afternoon, even in the dead of winter, around a pot-bellied stove. As long as two people get together who like to tell stories, baseball can be played anywhere.

Usually, the baseball story teller has a slight inclination to exaggerate. There is something exciting about a baseball story laced with the embellishment of 20 years or more even if it sometimes departs from the boundaries of truth.

The stories in this book are different. Some are strange, some are uncommon, some are almost unbelievable. Some are old, some have never been told before. Not all of the people in this book are famous. Some are like actors who have only one short line in a drama, then disappear and never appear again. These stories have only one thing in common: they actually did happen.

Getting these stories together required the help of other people. Those whose personal assistance or written material contributed most were Lowell Reidenbaugh of the *Sporting News*, Phil Howser of the Charlotte (N. C.) baseball club; Lee Allen of the Baseball Hall of Fame, Harold Kaese of Boston, Charles Einstein of San Francisco, Herbert Simon of *Baseball Digest* and Al Silverman of *Sport* Magazine. To all of them, and others who responded with willingness, I am grateful.

And if I have helped the reader learn to enjoy the "hot stove" game, then my purpose has been achieved.

Furman Bisher
Sports Editor
Atlanta *Journal*

1

Immortal by Accident

By the time he was nineteen years old, Stan Musial was playing his third season of professional baseball as a pitcher for the Daytona Beach Islanders in Florida. Although Daytona Beach did not play the best kind of baseball, Stan was happy doing the thing he loved—pitching. During his first two seasons in the minors Stan's wildness had held him back. At Daytona Beach, though, he had apparently found his control. By early August he had won seventeen games.

Then dawned what seemed to be the darkest day of Musial's life. His manager, Dickie Kerr, had discovered that Musial was also an effective hitter, and used him in the outfield many times when he wasn't pitching. On August 11, 1940, Musial was playing center field for the Islanders. He had pitched the night before.

With two out, a batter hit a sinking line drive in Musial's direction, and he made a run for the ball. He had often made shoetop catches, then hit the ground doing an intentional somersault. He wasn't showing off; Musial felt that it was the best way to protect his catch.

He made the catch on the run and turned his usual somersault. But somehow he miscalculated. As he hit the ground, he felt an awful pain in his pitching shoulder. He held on to the ball for the third out,

3

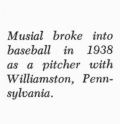

Musial broke into baseball in 1938 as a pitcher with Williamston, Pennsylvania.

but as he ran for the dugout he was clutching his shoulder. Dickie Kerr intercepted him near the third-base coaching box and asked if anything was wrong. Musial said it was only a slight pain that would soon go away. But it didn't. The shoulder ached all night as Stan fought to get to sleep. The next day Musial refused to tell Kerr that he was still in pain.

His turn to pitch came up two days later, and he accepted his assignment without a murmur. The opponent was Sanford, a strong team. The shoulder ached as he warmed up, and it ached as he pitched. He beat Sanford 5–4, but it was his last victory of the season.

Musial started again a few days later against Orlando. There was no escaping the terrible pain this time. It was more than he could bear. The Orlando team hit him hard, and he had to leave the game early.

Here he was, a young pitcher from steel-mill country, with a wife expecting a baby—and he himself had a bad arm. The situation looked hopeless to Musial. "Don't you think I ought to go home and find a job in the mills and forget baseball?" Musial asked Kerr the next morning.

"Not yet, Stan," Kerr told his young player. He had developed a fondness for the boy; he admired his good habits and his willingness as a player. Kerr had been a pitcher on the infamous Chicago Black Sox of 1919, the American League champions who sold out to gamblers in the World Series, agreeing to lose to the Cincinnati Reds. Kerr was one of the players who remained loyal to his team. He had won two games from Cincinnati. As a result, he had particular respect for a young man with character as well as talent.

Kerr told Musial that he was a good enough hitter to succeed even if his pitching arm didn't improve. To help the young player, Kerr invited Musial and his wife to live with him until their baby was born.

The Musials moved in with the Kerrs. When the

baby was born, the grateful young couple named him
Richard Kerr Musial. Although the pain soon disappeared in Musial's shoulder, full strength never did
return. But by the end of the season, he was able to
throw well enough to play in the outfield again.

The Daytona Beach team was a farm club of the
St. Louis Cardinals. When Musial's batting average
rose to .311, he was invited to the Cardinals' biggest
minor league camp the next spring. He reported as
a pitcher and worked with the pitchers until it became apparent that he could no longer compete
because of his bad arm.

One day the head of the Cardinal organization,
Branch Rickey, one of the most respected judges of
baseball talent, came out to watch the farm clubs play.
Musial was in the outfield although he still registered
on the camp roster as a pitcher.

After watching him only once at bat, Rickey
exclaimed: "That man's not a pitcher! He's a hitter!"

Mr. Rickey soon learned that Dickie Kerr had
already discovered Musial's hitting talent. Before the
season ended, Musial was playing for the Cardinals.
He moved rapidly through the minors from Daytona
Beach to Springfield, Missouri, to Rochester, New
York, and finally to St. Louis. He batted .379 at
Springfield and .326 at Rochester. During the last
weeks of the season he batted an amazing .426 for

Musial demonstrates the form that made him one of the sport's greatest hitters.

the Cardinals.

Musial retired after the 1963 season. He had led the National League in batting seven times, made 3,630 hits and 475 home runs, driven home 1,951 runs, and averaged .331 over a 22-season career.

Some of baseball's most exciting discoveries have been made by accident. Had it not been for that tumble he took on the night of August 11, 1940, one of the sport's greatest hitters might never have been found.

2
The Greatest Defeat

When Harvey Haddix of the Pittsburgh Pirates went out to warm up for the game against Milwaukee on the night of May 29, 1959, he felt sluggish. His fast ball didn't have its usual zing and his curve ball wasn't snapping the way a Haddix curve was supposed to snap.

He had been fighting a cold and had spent most of the day on the plane to Milwaukee. He wasn't exactly tired, but he was low on vitality.

"I don't feel sharp," he told his manager when he returned to the dugout. "I'll just have to do the best I can as long as I can."

At the end of nine innings, Haddix had not allowed a single Brave to reach first base: he had pitched a perfect regulation game. But the Pirates, although they had put men on base several times, had not been able to score against the Brave's pitcher Lew Burdette. So the game went into extra innings.

In the top of the tenth inning, the Pirates threatened. With one man on and one out, Dick Stuart, a dangerous slugger, came up as a pinch hitter. When he met one of Burdette's pitches, it looked and sounded like a home run. But the center fielder backed up against the fence and pulled it in. The next batter went out, too. The Pirates had failed again to give Haddix the one run he needed for victory.

Haddix kept his perfect game alive through the

9

The determined Haddix kept his perfect game alive through the tenth, eleventh and twelfth innings.

tenth, eleventh and twelfth innings. Thirty-six Braves had come to bat and gone out in order. The Braves' line-up was one of the most dangerous in the majors, including such sluggers as Hank Aaron, Ed Mathews, Joe Adcock and Del Crandall. Yet no one had received as much as a walk.

But the Pirates, who were much more successful at hitting the ball, were no more successful than the Braves in scoring. At the end of the Pirates' half of the thirteenth inning, there was still no score.

When Haddix came out to pitch in the bottom of

the thirteenth, Felix Mantilla, the Braves' second baseman was the first batter. He hit a sharp grounder to
the Pirates' third baseman, Don Hoak. In his hurried
effort to keep Haddix' perfect game alive, Hoak threw
low to first and Mantilla was safe on his error. The
next batter, Ed Mathews, sacrificed Mantilla to second.

Now the perfect game was gone and Haddix gave
Hank Aaron an intentional walk so that the Pirates
would have a chance for a double play. This brought
up Joe Adcock with men on first and second.

Although Adcock had struck out twice and
grounded out twice, he was one of the most dangerous hitters in the league. On the second pitch, he
swung and drove a fly into deep right-centerfield.
Center fielder Bill Virdon backed up all the way to
the wall, but the ball sailed just over his glove and
into the stands.

Now, Haddix' perfect game ended as a farce. Mantilla rounded third and came in with the winning run,
but Aaron, who thought that the ball was still inside
the park and that the game had ended when Mantilla
touched home, rounded second and then headed for
the dugout. Adcock continued on around the bases,
running out his home run.

The Braves, recognizing Aaron's mistake, rushed
him back out on the field where he touched second
base again and then completed his circuit of the bases.

Adcock followed him, touching each base behind him. But it was too late. The umpires ruled Adcock out for passing Aaron on the bases. Adcock's home run was changed to a double in the record books, although Aaron's run was allowed to score.

But the game had ended for Haddix when the first run scored. In three hours and nearly thirteen complete innings, he had struck out eight men, walked only one intentionally and allowed only one hit. His only mistake was one pitch to Joe Adcock.

"I knew I had a no-hitter," he said later in the clubhouse. "I could tell by the scoreboard. But the game had gone so long that I'd lost track of the innings and I wasn't sure if anybody had been on base or not."

Everyone left the park that night thinking the Braves had won 2–0 and it wasn't until the next morning that the official score was recorded. Warren Giles, president of the National League, ruled that the Braves had won by only one run. Since Adcock's hit had been scored a double, he said, it was not logical to count Aaron's run. Only Mantilla had legally scored and the score books were amended to read: Braves 1, Pirates 0.

But the change of score was little consolation for Haddix. He had pitched a magnificent game and yet had gone down in defeat.

After the disaster in the thirteenth inning, Haddix is consoled by Pittsburgh manager Danny Murtaugh.

3

The
One-Armed
Big Leaguer

Peter Wyshner was fascinated by trains. He would stand by the tracks near his house in Nanticoke, Pennsylvania, and watch the big engines tug their cargoes of freight and coal to distant places.

One day he had an urge to ride on one of the trains. When you're six years old, he thought, it's time to see some of the world. Soon a freight train came along on its way from Wilkes-Barre, seven miles away. It was moving slowly but it seemed fast to a six-year-old. As little Peter reached for the brakeman's ladder, his hand slipped and he fell into the path of the train. That night at the hospital, doctors decided to amputate the boy's right arm because it was so badly damaged.

From then on, Peter had to learn to live with only one arm. He had been naturally right-handed, and so he had to learn to write, eat and brush his teeth with his left hand.

When Pete began playing baseball, he discovered it was difficult to play with only one arm. How do you catch the ball and then throw it? How do you swing a bat and hit the ball? And how do you run? Few people realize that a runner's arms are important because they help him keep his balance.

Despite the difficulties, Peter played baseball whenever he got the chance. When he was ten years old, one of the sandlot teams in Nanticoke let him be the batboy. He got to watch good players almost every day and he learned much about the game. But he had to learn for himself how to overcome his handicap.

Then something happened that made Peter determined to become a good baseball player. Playing a "pickup" game one day, he slid hard into the catcher, a big, burly boy. The slide was so forceful that the ball was knocked out of the catcher's mitt.

The angry catcher got up snarling. "Why, if you had two arms I'd smash your nose," he said.

Peter became angry, too, and soon forced the catcher to take back his insult. He resolved to show the catcher and everyone else that he could outshine them all.

When he was old enough, he began playing for money on semiprofessional teams around Nanticoke. Players on semiprofessional teams work at a regular job during the week and play for the company team on evenings and weekends. He even changed his last name to Gray so that people could spell and remember it more easily. One Sunday he presented himself to Max Rosner, the man who operated the Bushwicks of Brooklyn, New York, one of the most famous semiprofessional teams in America.

"I can help your team, Mr. Rosner," Pete told him.

Max Rosner took one look at the one-armed man

and snapped back: "Is this your way of crashing the gate?"

Pete reached into his pocket and pulled out a ten-dollar bill. He didn't have much money, but he was willing to stake it on his ability.

"Take this," Pete said, "and if I don't make good, keep it."

Pete Gray eventually got his ten dollars back and became the Bushwicks' greatest drawing card. News of the one-armed player spread and people flocked to Dexter Park in Brooklyn to see Pete Gray. This pleased Pete, but he had even bigger ambitions. He wanted to play in the majors. And he knew that he would have to play for a professional team before the major leagues would even notice him.

Finally, in 1942, Mickey O'Neill, who managed a professional team at Three Rivers, Quebec, part of the Canadian-American League, said he would give Pete Gray a chance. O'Neill never regretted his decision. Pete batted .381 at Three Rivers, and if he hadn't broken his collarbone during the season, he would have qualified to lead the league.

Pete had learned to make catches in the outfield, and throw the ball to the infield. His movement was so swift that it could hardly be followed by the naked eye. He would catch the ball in a small, padless glove. Then he would flip the ball in the air while deftly removing the glove by sticking it under the stub of a right arm. As the ball came down, he caught it and made his throw.

Professional baseball in the United States was learning about Pete Gray's talents, too. In 1943, he played for the Memphis Chicks, members of the Southern Association, one of the toughest minor leagues.

His start was slow, and there were times when Memphis Manager Doc Prothro feared Gray would never make it. The fans came out to see him play, though, and soon Pete began to respond like a professional. By the end of the 1943 season, he was playing regularly and batting .289.

In 1944, Pete became the best player in the Southern Association. He batted .333, stole 68 bases, tying the league record, and was voted the Most Valuable Player. But he was happiest about the five home runs he hit. One thing a one-armed batter would seem to lack is power, and he felt that these five home runs made him a complete ballplayer.

One day during the season, a man brought a one-armed boy to the park to see Pete play. "I'll show you how Pete Gray plays baseball," Pete promised the boy before the game.

He did everything he had promised. He made eight catches in the outfield, fielding his position perfectly.

The game went into extra innings, and when Pete came to bat in the twelfth, with his team one run behind, he had already made four hits.

He faced the Nashville pitcher with grim determination. He got a pitch he liked and swung hard with his 36-ounce bat. It was a line drive that sailed over the leftfielder's head. By the time the ball reached the infield again, Pete was on third base with a triple.

Gray's was the first of two runs that Memphis scored in the twelfth, winning the game. Pete had shown his young admirer that there was a place for handicapped people even in baseball.

Pete's greatest thrill was yet to come. His ambition had been to play in the major leagues. Scouts from many teams had watched him play in Memphis. Some of them had recommended him. The eight league managers had endorsed him as a major league prospect. Still, he went home to Nanticoke after the season in doubt about his future.

It wasn't long before the doubt was erased. The St. Louis Browns announced that they had bought Pete's contract from Memphis for 20,000 dollars. This was especially gratifying because the Browns had just won the American League pennant.

Throughout spring training the next year, Pete was a quiet withdrawn member of the Browns. He couldn't be sure that baseball wanted him for his

*Until he proved himself with the Browns, one-armed Pete Gray was not
sure whether he was wanted for his ability or his oddity.*

ability rather than his oddity as a one-armed player.
Manager Luke Sewell, a compassionate man, had
tried to convince Pete that whatever job he earned
would be because of his ability.

Pete played infrequently when the season opened.
He was called upon for pinch-running, pinch-hitting
and an occasional appearance in the outfield. In mid-

May the New York Yankees came to Sportsman's Park in St. Louis for a major series of the home season. On a bright Sunday afternoon, the two teams met for a double-header before a crowd of 21,000.

Pete reached the park that day with the uneasy feeling that had become habitual with him in St. Louis. He was afraid that someday he might walk into the clubhouse only to be told that he was being sent back to the minors.

He was just buttoning up his uniform when he saw Manager Sewell walking toward him.

"Pete," said the manager, clapping his player on the back. "You're my new lead-off man. You'll be playing right field."

This was a great moment in Pete Gray's life— playing right field and leading off against the New York Yankees.

Pete showed his appreciation to Sewell and the Browns on the field that afternoon. He got on base five times, had four hits, drove in two runs, scored two runs and made nine plays in the outfield. The Browns beat the Yankees twice.

At last, Pete Gray realized his ambition—to be a real major leaguer.

4
One Last Game

Jim O'Rourke just couldn't give up baseball. He had begun playing the game in 1866 at the age of fourteen on the sandlots of his hometown, Bridgeport, Connecticut. Thirty-eight years later, he was still playing with the enthusiasm of a young man, even though he was over fifty.

Jim had attracted the attention of the Middletown (Connecticut) Mansfields, one of the teams in the new professional league, and joined them when he was barely twenty years old. He played first base for the Boston Red Sox and impressed spectators with plays that are routine nowadays—one-handed catches and line-drive snags. His popularity in Boston produced a string of clamoring children wherever he went. He was one of early baseball's best fielders and heaviest hitters. O'Rourke was something of a showman, too. Before games he would often engage in juggling stunts with the other infielders. During the next twenty-five years, he had played nearly two thousand games for the Boston, Providence, Buffalo, New York and Washington teams.

Jim was one of those men who just wanted to play baseball. By the end of his career, he had played nearly every position on some major league team. During his four years in Buffalo (when that team was in the majors), he was the manager as well. But O'Rourke particularly liked to catch and it was as a catcher that he played his last big league game.

When Washington gave him his release in 1893, Jim O'Rourke was forty-one years old. But he refused to give up baseball. Instead, to make sure that he had a place to play, he went back to Bridgeport and organized the Connecticut League. Then he formed his own team in Bridgeport as a member of the new league.

In 1904 Jim was still catching and managing the Bridgeport team. He was fifty-two years old and was also the secretary-treasurer of the Connecticut League. Furthermore, on days when the grounds-keeper failed to show up, which happened frequently, old Jim put the playing field in condition.

In New York, in the 1904 season, the New York Giants were about to clinch the National League Pennant. It was their first championship since 1889, when Jim O'Rourke had been one of their big stars. Nearby in Bridgeport, Jim followed the Giants closely. As the Giants approached the pennant-winning game, he had an idea.

On the day before the Giants were to play the game in which they could clinch the pennant, Jim took a train to New York. He approached John McGraw, manager of the Giants, and told him that he wanted to play one more time in the big leagues, if only for an inning.

McGraw was a manager of the old school. He ran his team with an iron hand and seldom gave in to sentiment.

"But Jim," he said to O'Rourke, "you're fifty-two years old."

"That doesn't make any difference," O'Rourke said. "I catch every day in Bridgeport."

"It's out of the question," McGraw said. "You ought to know better than to ask."

Jim continued to plead, but McGraw stood firm. The Giants were playing Cincinnati the next day for their one hundredth victory of the season as well as for the pennant. McGraw felt that this was no time for sentimental gestures.

O'Rourke then thought of another angle. He heard that "Iron Man" Joe McGinnity was to pitch for the Giants. He knew Iron Man and went to talk with him. Iron Man knew that Jim O'Rourke would be a good catcher, regardless of his age. So he agreed to talk to McGraw for O'Rourke.

"He just wants to catch an inning, Mr. McGraw," McGinnity said to his manager. "What can it hurt? It'll give him a big kick and the fans will like it, too. Besides, if we lose the game, we'll win the next one. We're not going to lose this pennant now."

Finally, McGraw gave in. The next afternoon at New York's Polo Grounds, the battery for the Giants was McGinnity and O'Rourke—and no prouder man than Jim ever wore a big league uniform.

The first inning went so well that when Jim returned to the bench he said, "I feel so good I think I'd like to catch another inning."

McGraw consented to let him stay in the game. Two innings became three and then Jim came to bat. The crowd cheered him because he reminded them of earlier Giant successes. He got a pitch he liked and lashed it into left field. Rounding first, Jim saw the left fielder bobble the ball. So he headed for second. The throw to second was wild, and Jim steamed into third.

That did it. The veteran from Bridgeport caught the whole game, never letting one of Iron Man McGinnity's pitches get by him or making a wild throw. The Giants won the game, their one hundredth victory and the pennant, and to Jim O'Rourke it was just like old times in 1889.

He went back to Bridgeport the next day flushed with success. One game was enough. He had proved that Jim O'Rourke could still catch for a big league team. After the Giants had won the pennant, he reminded his friends that he had helped to win the deciding game. He had been on his first pennant winning team in 1873—thirty-one years earlier.

Just to prove that he was no one-game flash in

the pan, Jim O'Rourke caught for five more seasons in Bridgeport before he finally let a younger man have his place. He retired from baseball in 1909 at the age of fifty-seven.

5
The Catcher Who Pitched All Night

Odell Barbary was never a famous player. He played only one game in the major leagues and never got a hit. He might have stayed in the majors much longer if he hadn't ruined his chances during a night game in Charlotte, North Carolina, in 1942.

Barbary was a catcher. By nature, he was a friendly country boy given to a lot of banter around the clubhouse. He was tall and lanky and had a long neck and strawberry-red hair. His teammates, the Charlotte Hornets of the Piedmont League, liked him because he could take a ribbing as well as he could hand one out.

On many occasions after a Charlotte pitcher turned in a sparkling performance, Barbary would needle him in his Southern drawl. "Man, you pitched tonight the way I used to pitch in high school," he would say. "It's a shame talent like mine has got to go to waste a-catchin'."

Some of the pitchers got angry, but most of them took it in good spirit. Barbary's boasting wasn't objectionable. For that matter, no one knew if he had ever pitched in his life. Therefore, few took him seriously.

One of the pitchers had a quick temper, however. "If you could catch as well as you say you can pitch," he said, "you'd be in the big leagues now."

Barbary only grinned and said, "I will be. You wait and see."

A few days before the end of the season, it happened. Barbary was bought by the Washington Senators and told to report for spring training the next year.

The pitcher began to press him now. "All right, big leaguer, now let's see you pitch."

"Aw, I hate to show you fellers up," Barbary replied.

By this time, the rest of the Hornets had joined in. They all wanted to see Barbary pitch.

In the game against Asheville on the final night of the season, Manager Harry Smythe gave his players a chance to play the position of their choice. Rising to his feet, Barbary said, "All right, gentlemen, you're going to see the great Barbary pitch tonight."

The Hornets cheered, and true to his word Barbary marched to the mound at Griffith Park in Charlotte. His pitching form wasn't very good, but he got the Asheville team out in the first inning with no trouble.

In the second inning, Asheville scored three runs. It was especially embarrassing when the Asheville pitcher, Larry Kempe, drove in two runs himself.

Barbary was unflustered, however, when he returned to the mound in the third inning. With the poise of a twenty-game winner, he shut out the Asheville team for two more innings. His teammates rallied in the fourth and tied the score, 3–3.

From this point on, Odell Barbary's pitching talent became a little more amazing each time he went out to pitch. The fifth, sixth, seventh, eighth and ninth innings went by and the score remained tied, 3 to 3.

In the tenth, it appeared that Barbary might be finished. Asheville put a runner on third base with only one out. But when the runner tagged up and tried to score on a fly to center field, the center fielder threw him out at the plate.

In the fourteenth inning, Charlotte had a chance to win. Charlotte's center fielder, the fastest runner in the league, singled and stole second. He moved to third on an infield out. But when he tried to score on a short fly to left field, he was cut down, in spite of his speed, by a good throw to the plate.

The fifteenth, sixteenth, seventeenth and eighteenth innings passed, and Barbary kept pitching. If anything, he was showing more style than at the beginning of the game, as if he was developing a rhythm. Fans who had been listening to a broadcast of the game began arriving at the park to see the miracle for themselves.

Finally, in the last half of the twenty-second inning, the end came suddenly. Charlie Roberts, the Charlotte shortstop, got a two-base hit. Smut Anderholt,

Odell Barbary boasted of his pitching ability, but no one took him very seriously.

who was playing third and had been to bat nine times without a hit, also doubled, and Roberts scored the run that made Odell Barbary the winning pitcher.

The catcher had pitched the longest game in the history of the Piedmont League. He had given up only eleven hits in twenty-two innings and scored the only two strikeouts of the game. But his boasting and his acceptance of his teammate's challenge were disastrous for him. Barbary ruined his great throwing arm that night, and with it he ruined his career.

Barbary was strangely humble in the clubhouse after the game that night. He said little and accepted congratulations with uncommon modesty. "I'll have to tell you the truth," he told his teammates after the crowd had retreated. "I never pitched a game before today in my life."

6
The
"Miracle Braves"
of 1914

Whenever sports comebacks are the topic of conversation the Boston Braves of 1914 are always mentioned. Saluting this determined team, Grantland Rice once wrote, "The Braves proved that no fight is hopeless."

Boston had finished fifth in the National League in 1913, to the severe displeasure of Manager George Stallings. Stallings was a hot-tempered Georgian who had no tolerance for defeat. One year he fired one of his players because he whistled a tune in the shower after losing a game.

"If a player is an easy loser," Stallings stormed, "I don't want him on my team."

Stallings always dressed in street clothes and wore out three or four pairs of trousers in a season, nervously sliding back and forth on the bench during the games. The 1914 season began on such a sour note that he was wearing out trousers as fast as his tailor could make them.

The Braves lost eighteen of their first twenty-two games and were unchallenged for last place. Baseball tradition says that the team in first place on July 4 will eventually win the pennant. But on July 4, the Braves were still last, fifteen games behind, and the New York Giants were leading the League.

As late as July 19, the Braves were still in eighth place. But Stallings had been making trades and the team was showing some new life. The Braves were

mostly players unwanted by other teams. Stallings
added to their reputation as rejects when he picked
up players from St. Louis, Philadelphia, Cincinnati
and Brooklyn.

But the cast-offs from other clubs were soon proving
their worth. By August, the Braves were really sailing.
On August 10, they moved into second place, breathing down the Giants' necks. In early September
they caught up with the Giants and passed them. In
a key game of the series in which they overtook the
Giants, the Braves won the hard way. They scored
three runs off Christy Mathewson, one of the greatest
pitchers of all time, and won in the last of the ninth
inning, 5–4.

The Braves were not to be stopped. In the second
half of the season, they won 60 games and lost only
16. They won the pennant by an amazing margin of
10½ games. But there was still a widespread tendency
to call their triumph a fluke.

It is true that the Giants had fallen into a slump
due to inferior pitching and the failure of some
established veterans to play up to their past per-
formances. But no one could deny that the Braves
had played sensationally during the last half of the
season. They probably would have been taken more
seriously had they not been opposing the Philadelphia
Athletics in the World Series.

Braves manager George Stallings, who always dressed in street clothes,
is seen here with Giant manager, John McGraw.

The Athletics were the "New York Yankees" of that day. Their line-up included five players who later were voted into the Cooperstown Hall of Fame: pitchers Herb Pennock, Chief Bender and Ed Plank; third baseman Frank "Home Run" Baker and second baseman Eddie Collins. Jack Barry played shortstop and Stuffy McInnis played first base, completing what was known as the "Hundred-Thousand-Dollar Infield." Manager Connie Mack was already considered one of the greatest managers of all time. He had won three of the four previous World Series.

Going into the 1914 World Series, then, the make-shift Braves were considered certain to lose to the vaunted American League champions. The National Leaguers found themselves the subject of ridicule, in spite of their dramatic rush to the pennant. When asked if he had scouted the Braves, Chief Bender reflected the feeling of the whole team with his sarcastic answer. "There's no need scouting a bush-league club like that."

There was some basis for the light regard in which the Braves were held. The catcher, Hank Gowdy, was only twenty-four and had never been a regular player before. The pitching staff had a decided lack of depth. For one of the pitchers, Bill James, this was his only good season. He won only 37 games in the majors, 26 of them in 1914.

Johnny Evers, the captain and shortstop, eventually made the Hall of Fame. But by 1914 he was a tired veteran having his last big moment. He never played a hundred games in a season again. The outfield was of such questionable quality that Stallings had used twelve men to play the three positions during the season and was still shuffling for the right combination in the World Series.

The first game was played in Philadelphia. The Braves' Dick Rudolph, a little right-hander weighing only 155 pounds, beat the Athletics and their famous pitcher, Chief Bender, 7–1. In the second game, James, who was to win only five more games in his major league career, beat the great Athletics pitcher Eddie Plank, 1–0, on a two-hitter. Afterward Mr. Mack coldly commented to Plank, "They play pretty well for bush leaguers, don't they, Eddie?"

As the teams switched from Philadelphia to Boston to resume the series, the Braves' clubhouse attendant asked Manager Stallings if he should leave the players' road uniforms in Philadelphia to save the trouble of transporting them back and forth.

"No," snapped Stallings. "We won't be coming back."

The opening game in Boston was one of the most thrilling World Series games ever played. The Braves' George Tyler faced the Athletics' Joe Bush, known

The Miracle Braves of 1914: 1. Gowdy, 2. James, 3 Evers, 4. Rudolph, 5. Tyler, 6. Connolly, 7. Moran, 8. Mann.

as "Bullet Joe," then only twenty-one years old.

The game went into extra innings, tied at 2–2. When the Athletics scored two runs in the top of the tenth, the outcome seemed certain. But as Grantland Rice wrote, "The Braves proved that no fight is hopeless."

Hank Gowdy, the Braves' young catcher, hit a home run to open the Braves' half of the inning. Then, Joe Connolly drove in Herb Moran on a sacrifice fly to tie the score 4–4. Boston fans were delirious.

The game wore on into the twelfth inning. In the Braves' half, Gowdy, who was having a tremendous series, came to bat. He hit a ground-rule double into the left-field bleachers and was then removed for a pinch runner, Les Mann. The next batter walked and Moran, the old cast-off from Cincinnati, laid down a bunt. "Bullet Joe" Bush pounced on the ball and had time to force Mann at third. But his hurried throw was wild, and Mann came home with the winning run. Final score: Braves 5, Athletics 4.

The fourth game was almost unnecessary. The proud Philadelphians were humbled and stumbling, desperately trying to regain their form. Stallings started Rudolph again, and by the fifth inning the little fellow had a 3–1 lead, which he carefully protected during the rest of the game.

Gowdy had batted .545, as well as winning fielding honors, and Rudolph and James had been the pitching stars. The mighty Athletics had lost four straight to Boston's "bush leaguers." It was the first time in modern baseball history that the losing team had not won at least one game. The miracle of the 1914 Braves was complete.

7
The Dog
That Made a
Box Score

A large Cuban baseball player named Roberto Gon-
zalo Ortiz appeared in Charlotte, North Carolina, in
1941, to play baseball for the Charlotte Hornets in
the Piedmont League. Ortiz loved to play baseball
and the Washington Senators, who owned his contract,
thought he played very well. He came as a pitcher
who had burning speed, but little control. When he
started to play for the Hornets, he was switched to
the outfield, where his strong arm would command
respect of base runners.

Because Ortiz could barely speak English, he found
himself alone in Charlotte except for one Cuban
friend and a small dog, who was the color of cooked
squash. The Cuban boy was shy but animals loved
him, especially his homeless mongrel dog. When the
team worked out, the yellow dog romped along with
Ortiz. When the team went into the clubhouse, he
seemed to wait especially for Ortiz to come out.
When the team played, the yellow dog seemed to
know that his place was out of the way.

Another thing the dog seemed to know was baseball. The excitement in the stands created when the
Charlotte team would work up a rally excited him,
too. Often the groundskeeper would be forced to
chase him out of the park.

One Sunday afternoon, though, while the yellow
dog was enjoying the freedom of the park, he com-

pletely forgot himself. Out of it he emerged as one of the most famous dogs in baseball lore.

The Charlotte team went to bat in the last of the ninth inning trailing by one run, apparently the victim of a tough pitcher. But the pitcher lost his control momentarily, and walked a Hornet batter. The next batter was Roberto Ortiz.

The big Cuban got a pitch that he liked and lashed into it. As he hit the ball, the crowd leaped to its feet with a roar. This aroused the yellow dog, who was sleeping in the dirt under the first-base bleachers. The ball had gotten by the center fielder and a run was scoring, tying the game. Ortiz would be trying for every base he could get.

As the Cuban neared first, he was joined by a sudden blur. The yellow dog, catching sight of his friend, had burst through the open clubhouse gate and was off to join him. Down to second base they went, the big Cuban and the little dog, running like a team. Then around second base, past the shortstop, whom the dog barely missed while making his wide turn.

The throw was coming in from the outfield now and Ortiz was in danger as he neared third. The coach signaled for him to slide and as Ortiz slid, the yellow dog slid, too. The umpire's hands flattened out in a safety signal. Both Ortiz and his dog had

Both Ortiz and his dog were safe at third.

made it.

How the game ended is really not important. What is important took place the next day. In the box score of the game, the Charlotte *News* made a special place for the little yellow dog. He appeared underneath Ortiz' name: "y—Yellow Dog." Below, in the space usually reserved for pinch hitters and pinch runners, appeared his explanatory line: "y—Yellow Dog ran with Ortiz in the 9th."

8
Corporal Brissie and Dr. Brubaker

Lou Brissie was seventeen years old and a freshman at Presbyterian College in South Carolina when the Japanese made their sneak attack at Pearl Harbor on December 7, 1941. The United States declared war, and immediately a fever to join the armed forces swept through college campuses. Brissie was one of those who felt the urge to volunteer.

But he had another ambition, too. He had always wanted to pitch for Connie Mack and the Philadelphia Athletics. Mack was the grand old man of baseball and had been the manager of the Athletics for more than forty years. Brissie's college coach, Eric McNair, a former Athletics shortstop, had seen Brissie pitch for the big mill team in his hometown, Ware Shoals, South Carolina, and had taken him to Philadelphia for a tryout with the Athletics. Brissie was tall and left-handed with a whip of a delivery in the style of the A's great Lefty Grove, who won three hundred games in the majors.

Mr. Mack had been impressed. But he advised Brissie to go to college and get an education. A contract with the Athletics would be waiting for him when he graduated. Mr. Mack even helped pay Brissie's college expenses, so the young man was especially eager to justify Mr. Mack's faith in him.

Then came World War II and Pearl Harbor; Brissie's guaranteed future began to collapse around him. Finally, in December, 1942, he could no longer resist the urge to enlist in the army.

"Coach, I've got to go," Brissie said to Eric McNair. "I'll be drafted sooner or later anyway. I want to go now so that I can get back to the Athletics and start pitching for Mr. Mack."

McNair knew that it would be of no use to try to stop him. Brissie was a boy of conscience and good judgment, and he had made up his mind.

Two years later, on December 7, 1944, in the Apennine Mountains of Italy, Corporal Lou Brissie and his fellow infantrymen were encamped near the city of Bologna. Brissie, now six feet, four inches tall and twenty years old, was leading a rifle squad on patrol.

Suddenly, with no warning, a self-propelled shell from German attackers struck near Brissie and his squad. Fragments flew everywhere, and not a member of Brissie's squad was left standing. Most of them were killed; the others were critically wounded.

How long he lay there, Brissie never knew. Slowly, though, consciousness returned. He could smell the acrid smoke that hung over the ravine in which he lay. He could see, though his vision was dull and shimmery, but he couldn't talk or move.

His first thoughts were of survival, and when a

searching party arrived this seemed assured. But the searching party started to pass him by. They thought he was dead, like the rest, and he couldn't cry out to let them know he was alive. He tried, but he had lost his voice, a temporary condition brought on by shock.

"Hey, that one moved!" one of the searching party said, taking one last glance at the mangled rifle squadsmen.

Somehow, through desperate effort, Brissie had moved his body enough to get one man's attention. Otherwise, he would have been left for dead. He had already lain in that muddy ravine for more than six hours, the shinbone of his left leg shattered by a piece of the shell, his body riddled with fragments. The fact that he had lived through the December chill and the loss of blood was a miracle in itself, but the miracles were only beginning.

At the battalion first-aid station, Brissie was given the first of forty blood transfusions. The next stop was the evacuation hospital in Naples, where Brissie woke up one morning to find a doctor bending over him, saying to an aide:

"This leg will have to come off."

Corporal Brissie now made the greatest stand of his life. Struggling into a leaning position on one elbow, he protested, "You can't take my leg off, doctor!

I'm a baseball player, and I've got to play ball."

The doctor, Major Wilbur Brubaker, was a serious man who seldom smiled or talked. By coincidence, he was also an ardent fan of the Cleveland Indians. Naturally, he had never heard of Lou Brissie, but the boy's determination convinced Brubaker to dedicate himself to making it possible for him to play baseball again.

There was not a piece of bone more than four inches long left in Brissie's leg. The idea that a pitcher as heavy as Lou would ever again be able to pivot and throw off the shattered leg seemed incredible but Major Brubaker offered him cautious encouragement. He warned Brissie, however, that complete recovery would take time and perseverance.

Putting Brissie's shattered leg back together again was like fitting together the pieces of a jigsaw puzzle. Major Brubaker used pieces of the fractured bone and wire and patience. He also had to fight the infection brought on by Brissie's long exposure to the cold.

After that it was a matter of one operation after another and one hospital after another for Corporal Brissie. First he went to the 300th General Evacuation Hospital in Naples. Then he was returned to the United States, where he was assigned to Finney General Hospital in Thomasville, Georgia. Next he went to Northington General Hospital in Tuscaloosa, Alabama, and finally he was transferred to Valley Forge General Hospital in Valley Forge, Pennsylvania.

He underwent twenty-three operations. But because of Major Brubaker's skill, the crisis had already passed and the leg had been saved. Strength was returning, though Brissie still had to use a crutch to get about. Since he was close to Philadelphia, he began to think about calling on Connie Mack and letting him know that his pitcher was on the way.

Throughout Brissie's time in the service, Mr. Mack had corresponded with him. After the battlefield injury, Mr. Mack's letters became more frequent and reassuring. "There will always be a place for you with the Athletics," Mr. Mack wrote soon after Brissie's brush with death. "Your first order is to recover and to keep your courage high. Then when you are well again, we shall have your uniform ready."

Mr. Mack's encouragement, Brissie's own desire to play baseball again and the faith of fellow patients who knew about his ambitions helped pull Lou through many periods of deep depression.

Finally the moment arrived. One morning in July, 1946, a tall, broad-shouldered young man with a crutch under his left arm presented himself at the offices of the Philadelphia Athletics. He said to the receptionist, "Tell Mr. Mack that Lou Brissie is here."

The uniform was ready, just as Mr. Mack had

promised. Brissie wore it that day and even warmed up with the bull-pen catcher. He stumbled about uncertainly and almost fell down trying to throw. The idea that this poor fellow would ever throw a baseball in the American League seemed absurd. Mr. Mack, however, patted him on the back and gave him more reassurance.

A few days later, Brissie returned to Valley Forge Hospital for another operation. An infection had been brought on by his exertion in Philadelphia. In the office of the Athletics, many thought they had seen the last of Lou Brissie as a baseball player.

Imagine their surprise when he arrived at their spring training camp in Florida the next year vibrantly healthy and ready to play. Over the damaged leg he now wore a steel brace and a lightweight shinguard similar to that worn by catchers. Although he was not as agile as most other players, he got about admirably for a man with only one good leg.

The Athletics had a farm team in Savannah, Georgia, and Mr. Mack decided that this was where his Purple Heart winner should break in. "You have shown me that you've got courage and you have shown me that you can pitch, Mr. Brissie," said Mr. Mack. "That's all I needed to know. One day you shall pitch for Philadelphia."

On opening day in the South Atlantic League in

Connie Mack's faith in Lou Brissie was justified when Lou signed a contract with the Athletics in 1948.

April, 1947, Lou Brissie was the starting pitcher for Savannah. At first things did not go well at all. The opposing team knocked him out of the box after four innings, but Savannah managed to win anyway.

Next came a defeat by Augusta, 3–0, and another defeat by Charleston, 1–0. Brissie was pitching well enough to win, and there was no doubt about the durability of the damaged leg, or his ability to perform on it. But his teammates just weren't hitting well enough.

In his fourth starting assignment, Brissie faced the Greenville team. Ware Shoals, Brissie's home town, is not far from Greenville, and that night many of his townspeople came to see him pitch. As he recognized old friends in the crowd, he filled with excitement.

Brissie beat Greenville that night and he didn't lose another game until July. Thirteen times in a row he won, and when the season was over, his record was 23 won and 5 lost. He had struck out 278 men in 254 innings, and achieved an earned run average of 1.91. He was the leading pitcher in the league in nearly every category.

In 1948 Philadelphia opened the American League season in Boston on Patriots Day. Connie Mack honored his returned war heroes by starting Phil Marchildon, a Canadian veteran, in the first game of

Lou was as determined on the pitching mound as he was on the battlefield.
He pitched successfully in the majors for six seasons.

the holiday double-header and former Corporal Lou Brissie in the second game. Marchildon pitched well and won a close game, 5–4.

The second game had been going only a few minutes when Brissie found himself pitching to one of the best hitters baseball had ever known—Ted Williams, the Red Sox left fielder. It was the first time Lou had ever seen the great Williams.

Although Brissie pitched carefully to him, the Red Sox slugger got a pitch he liked and rifled it back directly at the A's pitcher. Worse than that, the drive struck Brissie's leg with such force that the ball rolled all the way to the right-field fence.

Brissie fell as if he had been shot and players from both teams crowded around him. All of them were familiar with the story of the war hero's courageous fight to pitch again, as were thousands in the stands at Fenway Park.

Williams himself tagged base and anxiously joined the crowd around the fallen pitcher. Looking up from where he lay and spotting Williams' famous face above him, Brissie smiled broadly.

"Williams," he said good-naturedly, "I thought you were a pull-hitter."

A smile spread across Williams' face, too, and the anxiety was dispelled.

"I knew then," Williams said later, "that that guy

would make it."

The steel brace and the shinguard had saved the wounded leg. Suffering only a bruise, Brissie got up and pitched the entire game. He beat the Red Sox, 3–2.

It was the start of a good career with the Athletics. Brissie won fourteen games that season and sixteen the next season. He pitched in the majors for six full seasons. The ambition of a man who refused to give up on the battlefield, in the hospital or on the playing field had been fulfilled.

9
The Midget of St. Louis

One morning in August, 1951, Bill Veeck, president of the St. Louis Browns, called a theatrical agent in Chicago and said, "Marty, I want you to find me a midget who's athletic and game for anything."

A few days later, Eddie Gaedel showed up in Veeck's office in St. Louis. Gaedel met all Veeck's specifications. He stood just three feet, seven inches tall, weighed only sixty-seven pounds and was athletically inclined. Veeck told Gaedel his plan, and found that the midget was quite willing to go through with it.

Veeck, who formerly operated the Cleveland Indians and later the Chicago White Sox, was known for his odd publicity schemes. He had used clowns in the coaching box. He had introduced Satchel Paige, a famed Negro pitcher, to the major leagues at the age of forty-eight, when most players have retired. He had awarded a ton of coal, a barrel of oysters and a billy goat as gate prizes.

After they had discussed Veeck's plan, Veeck sent Gaedel home to Chicago and told him to be back in St. Louis on Aug. 18. On that date, the Browns, the eighth-place team in the league, were playing the Detroit Tigers, the seventh-place team. Eighteen thousand fans were attracted to Sportsman's Park by a special day dedicated to one of the Browns' radio sponsors. Any fan could have detected on his score-

59

Bill Veeck (right) bought the Browns from Bill DeWitt (left), only a month before he introduced his midget to beef up the poor attendance.

card the addition of a player listed as "1/8: Gaedel." For some reason or another, few of them did. To those who did notice it, it looked like a typographical error.

Meantime, Veeck and his chief assistant, Bill Durney, had signed Gaedel to a formal American League player contract. In the secrecy of their office, they had schooled the midget in the technique of batting. And they had ordered the construction of a huge make-believe cake, supposedly as a part of the tribute to the radio sponsor.

A double-header was scheduled that Sunday afternoon. At the end of the between-games ceremony, the make-believe cake was rolled up to home plate. Out of the cake emerged Eddie Gaedel, dressed in an authentic St. Louis player uniform with the fractional number "1/8" on his back. To complete the costume, he wore a pair of elves' shoes turned up at the toes. He was a real, live Brownie.

Gaedel carried a toy bat, but no one suspected what was about to take place until the public-address announcer introduced the lead-off batter for the Browns in the last half of the first inning.

"Now batting for Saucier," he said in his ball-park baritone, "number 1/8, Gaedel."

Out of the St. Louis dugout strode Eddie Gaedel, carrying the toy bat on his tiny shoulder. The astonished umpire, Ed Hurley, took off his mask and called for the St. Louis manager, Zack Taylor.

"Hey, Zack," Hurley said, "what do you think you're doing? Is this some kind of joke?"

With a straight face, Taylor pulled an American League contract from his pocket showing that Eddie Gaedel had been duly signed to play for the St. Louis Browns at a salary of one hundred dollars a game. There was nothing Hurley could do but allow the midget to take his turn at bat.

Bob Swift, the Detroit catcher, called time. Bewildered, he walked to the mound and stood scratching his head as he and the Detroit pitcher, Bob Cain,

It was impossible for Detroit pitcher Bob Cain to pitch into a 1½ inch strike zone.

discussed the problem of pitching to a midget. Veeck had already measured Gaedel's "strike zone." It was 1½ inches high when Gaedel took the normal batting stance.

Veeck had ordered Gaedel not to swing at a pitch under any condition. Realizing that no pitcher could throw three strikes through a 1½-inch zone, Veeck only wanted Gaedel to get a walk. Even without swinging at a pitch, he would bring national attention to the Browns, who were the poorest members of the American League, both in dollars and talent.

Gaedel was nervous as he stepped into the batter's box. He timidly took a stance in the left rear corner of the right-hand batting rectangle. Cain, a right-handed pitcher, still wore an expression of astonishment as he prepared to pitch. Catcher Swift unconsciously added to the hilarity of the situation by getting down on both knees behind the plate.

Cain's first pitch was a serious attempt at a strike. It sailed high over Gaedel's head. So did the second.

Now Cain was laughing. The next two pitches were just medium-hard lobs three feet over the midget's head. The little batter threw down his toy bat in the best professional manner and trotted down to first base.

Time was called while a pinch runner, Jim Delsing, was sent into the game for him. Again in the character of a professional player, Gaedel slapped Delsing across his rump as his replacement relieved him on first base.

Gaedel ran off the field, into the St. Louis dugout and out of the major leagues for life while 18,000 fans roared with laughter at the comedy they had witnessed.

The event had its repercussions. But despite complaints from baseball executives and some newspapers, Bill Veeck's publicity stunt was successful. He had brought badly needed attention to the St. Louis Browns, and he had brought off an act that will be talked about as long as baseball is played in America.

Eddie Gaedel had, in his own small way, also achieved the fame he sought. He would always be known as the only midget who ever played in the major leagues. Even Frank Saucier had set some kind of record. He was the only major leaguer ever to be taken out of a game for a midget.

10
Dusty Rhodes Breaks Up the Series

Leo Durocher once said that Dusty Rhodes was the craziest looking ballplayer he had ever seen. He wore his cap at a cockeyed angle. He ran with the speed of a weary blacksmith. His fielding was very uncertain. And for a throwing arm, he might as well have been using a rubber band. But he could hit.

Because Dusty Rhodes could hit, the New York Giants, managed by Durocher, won the National League pennant in 1954. At the two most critical points of the season, in a series against the Brooklyn Dodgers, it was Rhodes' pinch hits that led the Giants to victory. Playing mostly as a pinch hitter and a reserve outfielder, Rhodes went to bat only 164 times during the regular season. But he hit 15 home runs and drove in 50 runs while compiling an average of .341.

But this was only the warm-up for the grand finale. In the 1954 World Series the Giants met the Cleveland Indians. The Indians had a team of historic strength, including Early Wynn, Mike Garcia, Bob Lemon and the great Bob Feller as starting pitchers and the best relievers in the major leagues—Ray Narleski and Don Mossi. They had won 111 games during the season, a record for the American League.

The Giants were not a spectacular team, but they were well balanced. Johnny Antonelli and Sal Maglie were the pitching stars and Willie Mays, Al Dark and

Don Mueller lead the offense. Dusty Rhodes was in reserve.

The series began in New York, and the Indians were favored to beat the Giants on the strength of their pitching. Lemon, who had won twenty-three games during the regular season, was facing Maglie, who had won only fourteen. Cleveland scored two runs in the first inning, but the Giants tied the game in the third. From that point until the tenth inning, it was a pitchers' duel. In the eighth inning, Willie Mays saved the Giants from defeat when he made a spectacular catch against the wall in center field. Two Indians were on base at the time and would almost certainly have scored if Mays had missed the ball.

When the Giants came up in the last half of the tenth, the score was still 2–2. Mays walked and stole second. Hank Thompson was walked intentionally. It was Monte Irvin's turn to bat when Durocher put in his first call for Rhodes to pinch hit.

Rhodes came out of the dugout with his slew-footed walk, swinging an armful of bats. He stepped in to face Lemon and looked at only one pitch. He knocked it into the right-field bleachers at the Polo Grounds, driving in three runs. The Giants won, 5–2.

In the second game, Cleveland led 1–0 going into the Giants' half of the fifth inning. Mays walked and Thompson reached base behind him on a single.

Dusty is being congratulated on his 10th-inning three-run homer in the 1954 Series against the Indians.

Irvin would be up next. As Durocher recounted it later, "I looked down the bench and there was Dusty, already up with a bat in his hand. He didn't say anything, but his eyes said, 'Put me in, Skip. I'm ready.' And so I put him in."

This time Rhodes faced Early Wynn, who was then at the peak of a fine career. He slapped a single into right field, scoring Mays. Thompson scored later, and the Giants led, 2–1.

After batting for Irvin, Rhodes went to left field in Irvin's place. Coming to bat in the seventh inning, Dusty gave the Giants a safe lead with a smashing home run that hit the facing on the upper deck of the Polo Grounds.

The Series moved to Cleveland for the third game, where Mike Garcia faced Ruben Gomez of the Giants. The Giants got to Garcia early, with singles by Dark and Mueller opening the third inning. An intentional walk loaded the bases, and Irvin was due at bat. It was early, but there was little hesitation now. Rhodes was up with a bat in his hand again. This time he needed only one pitch. He drove another single into right field, scoring two runs. The Giants won again 6–1.

The next day the Giants took the Series from the Indians with their fourth straight victory, completing one of the great upsets of the year.

Durocher managed to win the fourth game without calling on Rhodes. But the confident utility man had already done enough for one World Series. In six times at bat, he delivered four hits for an average of .667. He hit two home runs and drove in seven runs. Three of his hits and one of his home runs had come when he was a pinch hitter.

This incredible record marked the pinnacle of a short-lived baseball career. After the series Rhodes was acclaimed one of the game's most exciting performers and yet three years later, at the age of thirty, he was back in the minor leagues. But for one four-game World Series there has never been a hotter man with a bat than Dusty Rhodes.

11

A Game of Records

The World Series of 1920 set a number of records. First, Cleveland had never played in a modern World Series. Their opponents, the Brooklyn Dodgers, had played in the series just four years earlier but had been in the second division ever since. It was a surprise that the two teams were there at all. But it was the fifth game that kept the record keepers busy.

Twenty-six thousand fans crowded into old League Park in Cleveland to see the two teams play that day. The Series was tied at two victories apiece. Each manager was starting his pitching ace: Burleigh Grimes for Brooklyn and Jim Bagby for Cleveland. Grimes had beaten Bagby in the second game so Bagby was particularly eager to win the rematch.

From the first inning the Indians began giving Grimes double trouble. The first two Indian batters reached base on singles. Then, Tris Speaker, the Indians' player-manager laid down a bunt, and as Grimes attempted to field it, he fell flat on his back. The bases were loaded with nobody out when Elmer Smith came to bat. Some fans were still trying to find their seats in the midst of this hubbub. Smith had batted over .300 in 1920 for the first time since 1914 when he had appeared in only 13 games.

Grimes bore down on the Indian batter, who swung at the first two pitches and missed. The third pitch was outside as Grimes "wasted" one, and Smith let

Elmer Smith

it go by. But the fourth pitch was a fast ball that
was just what Smith had been waiting for. He swung
and the ball disappeared over the right-field screen.

The three base runners spun around the bases,
followed by Elmer Smith, who had done something
no other player had ever done. It was the first grand-
slam home run hit in a World Series. To prove that
it was no simple feat, thirty-three years passed before
Mickey Mantle of the Yankees hit the next series
grand-slammer against the Dodgers in 1953.

Grimes was still pitching as the fourth inning
began. The Indians threatened again. The lead-off
man, Doc Johnston, got a hit, took second on a passed

ball and went to third on an infield out. Steve O'Neill, the catcher, was walked because Bagby, who was the next batter, was a weaker hitter and Grimes figured he could handle him. Instead, Bagby slammed a drive into right-center field that fell into the bleachers for a three-run home run, the first home run ever hit in a World Series by a pitcher.

By the fifth inning, Grimes had disappeared from the game. The merciless Indians had hammered him for nine hits and seven runs, including the two historic home runs and a triple. Working with such a comfortable lead, the Indians' Bagby seemed to let up in the fifth. The first two Dodger batters, Pete Kilduff and Otto Miller led off with singles, bringing up Grimes' replacement, pitcher Clarence Mitchell. With runners on first and second and no one out, the Dodger manager was willing to allow his pitcher to bat rather than call on a pinch hitter. In fact, he felt so much confidence in Mitchell that he flashed the hit-and-run sign, meaning that both Kilduff and Miller were to be off and running as Bagby released his pitch.

Mitchell met the ball squarely for what seemed to be a certain hit over second base. Since Dodger base runners were moving, Wambsganss, the Indian second baseman, ran toward second base to cover on the play. With an acrobatic leap, Wambsganss speared the line drive for one out. Suddenly he

Bill Wambsganss.

found himself faced with the play of a lifetime.

Kilduff, who had been on second base, was already nearing third. Wambsganss stepped on second base, forcing Kilduff out for the second out. Miller, who had been on first base, was nearing second when he realized what was happening and came to a dead stop. Wambsganss simply put the tag on him for the third out. He had completed the first and only unassisted triple play in World Series history.

It was no more Mitchell's day at bat than it had

been Grimes' day on the mound. The next time the Brooklyn relief pitcher came to bat, a teammate was on first base. He hit another smashing ball, this time on the ground, to Wambsganss, who promptly turned it into a double play. In two times at bat, Mitchell had been responsible for five of his team's outs. This was another first in a World Series.

Five victories were required to win a World Series in those days. The Dodgers were so thunderstruck by the Indians' performance in the fifth game that they never recovered. They lost that day, 8–1, and never scored another run as the Indians shut them out twice and completed the Series in two more days.

12

Ol' Diz
Makes a
"Comeback"

In the mid-1930s, Dizzy Dean was one of the greatest pitchers baseball had ever seen. But by 1938, he was through. The St. Louis Cardinals, for whom he had had his biggest years, had traded him to the Chicago Cubs. The Cubs used him sparingly in 1938, just enough to help them win the pennant, but he was pitching with his heart and his head. His fast ball was gone.

Dean struggled through two more seasons with the Cubs, then suffered the humiliation of being sent down to the minor leagues. The best he could do with Tulsa in the Texas League was to break even, winning eight and losing eight.

This was the final confirmation. Even Dean was forced to admit that he was through, and when the St. Louis Browns asked him to become their radio broadcaster in 1941, Dean accepted gladly. Talking had always been one of his strong points, but he usually talked about himself.

Talking about others was the unnatural part of baseball broadcasting for Dean, but in his unique way he learned to keep his listeners entertained. His grammar was so bad, however, that school teachers complained about his broadcasts. They said that he was a bad influence on their students. Although his use of the English language never improved, Dean did make himself valuable to the Browns, who were consistently the worst team in the American League.

Surprisingly, the Browns improved enough to win their first pennant in 1944, during World War II. But when the soldiers and sailors began returning home, strengthening the other teams in the league, the Browns slipped back into the second division. By 1947 they were dragging along in last place and attracting few fans to Sportsman's Park.

Bill DeWitt, president of the Browns, asked Dean to talk up the good plays the Browns made and keep their minds off the bad ones.

"Doggone it, Mr. DeWitt," Dean replied, "they just ain't making many good plays that I can talk about, but I'll try."

Try as he would, however, Dean frequently had to talk more about bird dogs, country recipes and country ballads than about the good plays the Browns were making. One day he became so disgusted with the Browns' pitchers that he blurted out: "Whatsa matter with these guys? Their fast balls wouldn't break a pane of glass. Doggone if I know what this game's comin' to. I'll bet I could beat nine out of ten of these guys that call theirselfs pitchers these days."

Among those listening to the broadcast were the wives of the Browns' pitchers. All of them were anxious about the welfare and reputations of their

Dizzy's remarks about the Browns' pitching angered the pitchers' wives.

husbands. They began calling President DeWitt and complaining.

"If that Dean thinks he's so great," they said, "why doesn't he get out there and pitch himself?"

DeWitt decided that the wives had a good idea. Attendance at the Browns' games was so low and debts were so high that he was willing to try anything that might bring out a crowd at Sportsman's Park.

He called Dean in.

"How would you like to pitch a game for the Browns, Diz?" asked DeWitt.

"I knowed that's what you wuz callin' me about," Dean said. "These females have been wearing me out on the telephone. I'm ready. When do I pitch?"

Dean went through the formality of signing a contract, which is necessary before appearance in a major league game. Then, on the afternoon of September 28, he left his broadcasting booth to pitch for the Browns. This was seven years after his last full season in baseball.

Dean faced the Chicago White Sox and, as DeWitt had expected, a crowd of 16,000 turned out for a game that normally would have drawn about 2,000. Don Kolloway, the White Sox first baseman, was the first batter Dean faced, and he lined a single into the outfield. The next batter hit into a double play and the third batter grounded out. Dean had survived the first inning.

In the second inning Dean gave up a single and a walk with one out. The wives of the Browns' pitchers must have been delighted. It looked as if Dean was about to be repaid for his unkind remarks about their husbands. But crafty old Diz had a few good pitches left. He kicked his left leg a little higher, reared back a little farther and threw to the

Seven years after his last full season the Diz showed his old form again.

next batter. The batter hit a grounder to the short-stop, who flipped to second, starting another double play and ending the inning.

In the third inning, Dean put the White Sox down in order—Mike Tresh, Ed Lopat and Kolloway. Now it was time for Dizzy himself to come to bat. As Dean came down the dugout steps, Dutch Hofmann, one of the Browns' coaches, said, "Are you all right, Diz, or should I put a pinch hitter in for you now?"

"You're doggone right I'm all right," Dean told Hoffmann. "Where's my bat?"

Dean went to the plate swinging a red-striped bat made especially for him. When Pitcher Lopat of the White Sox delivered the ball, he swung. It was a hit, a line-drive single to left field. On the way to first, though, Dean pulled a muscle in his leg.

He did his best to cover up as he went back to the mound for the fourth inning, but he was plainly favoring the injured leg. The first batter singled, but Diz retired the next three. Even so, when he walked off the mound at Sportsman's Park at the end of the inning, he knew he'd pitched his last game.

"I guess I better let somebody else pitch, Dutch," Dean told Hofmann. "This leg of mine is about to kill me."

But Dean had proved his point. He had faced only fourteen batters in four innings, two above minimum, and had held the White Sox scoreless. The Browns didn't win, unfortunately. A relief pitcher lost the game in the ninth inning, but the defeat had nothing to do with Dizzy Dean.

"I said I could pitch as good as most of these fellers," Dean told newspapermen that day, "and I can. But I'll be doggoned if I'm gonna ever try again. Talking's my game now, and I'm just glad that muscle I pulled wasn't in my throat."

13

The One-Inning Home Run King

The *Official Baseball Guide* for 1930 shows that during that season a player named Gene Rye hit twenty-six home runs for Waco, Texas. But the record doesn't show that Rye, in that same season, also had the biggest inning a batter has ever had in professional baseball.

Rye's real name was Eugene Mercantelli. But before he left his home in Chicago to try his hand at the game, a friend convinced him that a long name like Mercantelli would never fit into a newspaper headline or a box score. So he changed his name to Gene Rye. Gene was almost as short as his new name, but he was a strong little man and his bowed legs gave him good balance in the batter's box.

Night baseball had just come to Waco in 1930, so when the club scheduled a night game on August 6, there was a good crowd at the stadium. An even larger audience followed the game by radio, for this was the first night game broadcast in the Texas League.

When Gene Rye reached the ball park that night, he felt no better or worse than usual. He had had a good season at Waco. He was batting among the league leaders and he had hit nearly twenty home runs. He was almost certain to be bought by a team in a higher league at the end of the season. Perhaps even the major leagues would be interested.

That night Waco was playing the Beaumont, Texas, team. Going into the eighth inning, Waco was behind, 6–2, and the Beaumont pitcher, Jerry Mallet, showed no signs of losing his sharpness.

Rye was the first batter of the inning for Waco, and he hit Mallet's second pitch over the right-field fence for a home run. One home run should not have affected the Beaumont team since they still had a three-run lead, but it seemed to affect Mallet. He gave up a walk, a single and another walk to the next three batters. Waco now had enough runners on base to tie the score, and Mallet was taken out.

A pitcher named Ed Green relieved him, but Green was no improvement. Waco not only tied the score, but runs began pouring across the plate as if a dike had broken. By the time the Beaumont manager called time again, seven runs had scored and there was not even one out. He brought in a third pitcher, Walter Newman.

The first batter Newman faced was Gene Rye. There were two men on base when Rye stepped in to bat for the second time in the inning. The swarthy little outfielder swung his bat, met Newman's pitch with a loud crack and sent another drive over the right-field fence.

Now ten runs had scored and Beaumont had not retired one Waco batter. They finally got one man out, but the parade of batters continued. Another player, Tony Piet, later an infielder with several major league teams, hit a home run. Then Pitcher Newman struck out a Waco player named Sanguinet for the second out. But the two outs weren't enough to keep Gene Rye from making a third appearance before the end of the inning. This time the bases were loaded. The crowd sat forward in the stands, eager to see what would happen.

The first pitch was a ball. With the bases loaded, Newman took a long windup. Then he threw again. Rye met the ball solidly and the fans jumped to their feet. The ball sailed over the head of the center fielder, over the fence in center field and out of the park, farther than either of the other two home runs.

By the time the inning ended, Waco had scored eighteen runs. Gene Rye had hit three home runs and driven in seven runs. In the press box, sports writers searched the pages of their record books to find another professional player who had ever hit three home runs in one inning, but found none. And no professional player since 1930 has equaled Gene Rye's performance.

Later that season the Boston Red Sox bought Rye's contract for 1931. Due to a knee injury, his career with the Red Sox lasted only seventeen games, however, during which he never hit a home run. There

was no place for him in the big league sun, but down
in Waco, Texas, they continued to talk about Gene
Rye—the man who swung a bat for one inning as no
one has swung one before or since.

*n August 6, 1930, Gene Rye swung a bat for one inning as no one ever
ıs—before or since. He is shown here with the Red Sox, who bought his
ntract that season.*

14

The Day the Tigers Struck

The most untalented, unbelievable team that ever played major league baseball took the field in Philadelphia on May 18, 1912. The players wore the uniforms of the Detroit Tigers, but it didn't take close inspection to reveal that there wasn't a real Tiger in the group.

This team took the field as a result of the only strike that has ever been held in the major leagues. The strike had developed two days earlier in New York. On May 16, the Tigers played the New York Highlanders (later called the Yankees) in New York City. During the game, the constant heckling of one Highlander fan began to get on the nerves of the Tiger's hot-tempered star, Ty Cobb.

Once during the game, Cobb went to Harry Wolverton, manager of the Highlanders, and said, "There's going to be trouble if that fellow isn't stopped."

It is the home team's responsibility to maintain order in any park. But Cobb was given no assurance that measures would be taken to silence the man.

Finally, as Cobb was nearing his boiling point, the fan launched into another great outburst. Cobb sprinted for the stands, leaped the rail and picked out the abusive fan. By the time bystanders separated the men, the heckler was seriously cut and bruised.

Ban Johnson, president of the American League, suspended Cobb indefinitely without a hearing for

Cobb's suspension caused a Tigers' sympathy strike.

his behavior. But the Detroit players backed Cobb unanimously and sent Johnson the following telegram.

Feeling Mr. Cobb is being done an injustice by your action in suspending him, we, the undersigned, refuse to play in another game until such action is adjusted to our satisfaction. He was fully justified, as no one could stand such personal abuse from anyone. We want him reinstated or there will be no game. If players cannot have protection, we must protect ourselves.

Detroit had an open date between the Highlander game and their game with Philadelphia on May 18. Meanwhile, Johnson came to Philadelphia from his office in Chicago and threatened the entire Detroit ball club with suspension if the players refused to take the field against the Athletics. Johnson also threatened the owner of the Tigers with a $5,000 fine for every game his team missed. To avoid the fine in case his team still refused to play, the owner instructed his manager, Hughey Jennings, to round up a standby team.

On May 17, word was passed around Philadelphia that Detroit was seeking a standby team. On the morning of May 18, an assortment of college and sandlot ballplayers showed up at the Aldine Hotel, Tiger headquarters in Philadelphia, hoping to play for the striking Tigers.

The hopeful recruits filed by in a long line while Jennings cut the "squad" by tapping good prospects on the shoulder. He interviewed them briefly and selected eighteen to fill the Detroit uniforms. He had a full squad ready in case the regular Tigers carried out their strike threat.

On the afternoon of May 18, the regular Tigers left their hotel rooms, went by taxi to Shibe Park, home of the Athletics, and suited up. Their spokesman, Jim Delahanty, asked the umpire in chief:

"Has Cobb's suspension been lifted?"

When the umpire told him it hadn't, the Tigers went back to the dressing room, removed their uniforms and returned to the hotel. The first and only major league baseball strike had begun.

At game time, Manager Jennings put his emergency team on the field. A young theology student from St. Joseph's College named Al Travers was selected to pitch. The third baseman was a local boxer who had reversed the letters of his last name, Graham, and was known as Billy Maharg.

Two loyal Tiger coaches were pressed into service, Joe Sugden and James McGuire. Sugden was forty-two years old and he had broken into the big leagues nearly twenty years before. He played first base. McGuire was approaching fifty and had been a player and manager in the majors for thirty years. He was the catcher. The rest of the team was filled out by students from St. Joseph's and Georgetown University and sandlotters from around Philadelphia.

The true identity of the player who filled Cobb's shoes in center field was not known for many years. All that came out in the newspaper box scores the next day was this abbreviation: "L'n'h's'r, cf." The man's name was Leinhauser and he later became a police officer in Philadelphia.

But anonymity was just as well for "L'n'h's'r" and all the others because the substitute Tigers were devastated. Jack Coombs, the pitching ace of the Athletics, started the game. He was succeeded in early innings by another pitcher named Boardwalk Brown, who allowed the pickups their only two runs of the game, produced chiefly by the two old coaches, Sugden and McGuire, who had one hit apiece, and a sandlot player named Irwin, who hit two triples in three times at bat.

Meanwhile, the Athletics scored at least two runs in every inning except the second and fourth. Eddie Collins, the Hall of Fame second baseman, made five hits and scored four runs. Amos Strunk, the center fielder, made four hits, including a double and a triple.

In the end, the Athletics got 25 hits off the unfortunate Travers and won the game 24–2. Travers, who later became a Roman Catholic priest, set a major league record by allowing 24 runs to score. It wasn't all his fault though: nine errors by his teammates accounted for ten unearned runs.

After the game, the problem of the strike still had to be solved. It was obvious that Detroit couldn't afford to put such an inept team on the field again, and there was another game to be played the next day. The striking Tigers weren't budging and Johnson remained firm.

Newspapermen from all over the league rushed to the scene to cover the story. In New York the *Daily American* conducted a poll among its readers, asking them if they favored Cobb or the League President. The vote resulted in a landslide for Cobb: 3,013 to 1,167. Mail poured in from aroused fans. Many who had been sitting close to the abusive fan in Highlander Park wrote of their sympathy for Cobb.

Finally, Cobb himself broke the deadlock. When it became clear that neither Johnson nor the Tigers would give in, Cobb went to his teammates and said:

"Boys, the principle of this thing has been entirely open to the public. I'm going to ask you to forget me and go back.

"I don't want you paying fines and one of the conditions of your going back should be that no fine will be enforced on any of you. I'll be all right. They'll let me come back sometime soon, so please go back and play tomorrow."

As soon as Johnson reduced Cobb's suspension to ten days and established his fine at fifty dollars, the Detroit players returned to duty.

Of the substitute players, only Billy Maharg ever appeared in another major league game. Four years later, he played another one-day stand as an outfielder for the Philadelphia Phillies.

15
Connie Mack's Big Gamble

In 1929 Howard Ehmke of the Philadelphia Athletics was thirty-five years old and in the shadows of a substantial career as a big league pitcher. He had won 166 games and pitched in more than 400 games for Detroit, Boston and Philadelphia in the American League during a career of thirteen seasons. Ehmke had a hunch that his playing days were about to come to an end when Manager Connie Mack called him into his office one morning.

The Philadelphia team was preparing to leave on its last Western trip of the season. They were in first place and running strong. But Mr. Mack told Ehmke that morning that he could pass up no chance to keep his team at top strength. He needed a place on the roster for a young pitcher. And to make room, Howard would have to go.

Ehmke understood the problem. He had pitched in only eleven games all season and knew that he could not take much credit for the Athletic's fine performance. It was likely that a younger man could do more for the team. But Ehmke had one favor to ask.

"I've always wanted to pitch in a World Series," he told Mr. Mack. "And if this is going to be my last season, I'd like to work in this one, if only for a couple of innings. I think I've got one more good game left in this arm of mine."

99

Mr. Mack studied the old pitcher. The Chicago Cubs were leading the National League by a good margin and would probably be the Athletics' rivals in the World Series. While the Athletics were going. West, the Cubs were coming East for series with the Phillies and the Giants.

"All right, Howard," Mr. Mack said. "While we're out West, you follow the Cubs. Watch them play the Phillies and the Giants. See what they like to hit and what their weaknesses are. Don't let anybody know what you're doing. When the World Series comes up, we're going to give everybody a big surprise."

Both the Athletics and the Cubs held their leads and won their pennants as expected. The World Series opened in Chicago on October 8, and it was assumed that Mr. Mack would start one of his pitching aces, George Earnshaw, who had won 24 games that season, Lefty Grove, who had won 20, or Rube Walberg, who had won 18. Even the Philadelphia players were surprised when Howard Ehmke, the fading veteran, began to take his warm-up pitches in front of their dugout before the game.

Ehmke had pitched only fifty-five innings and won only seven games during the season. Everybody in baseball thought he was through. Yet, Mr. Mack dared to start him against one of the hardest-hitting

ᴐnnie Mack knew baseball talent and gave Ehmke a last chance for glory.

teams that had ever come into a World Series. The Chicago line-up included hitters such as Rogers Hornsby, who had won the National League batting crown with an average of .380 and was voted the League's Most Valuable Player; Hack Wilson, who batted in 159 runs during the season and had a .345 average; Riggs Stephenson, who hit .362; and Kiki Cuyler, who ended the season at .360.

Mr. Mack was gambling with Ehmke but he knew baseball talent and believed that the veteran could win the game. Besides, if Ehmke did lose, the Athletics still had the rest of their fine pitching staff in reserve.

Ehmke retired the Cubs in order in the first inning and finished off the second by striking out Stephenson and Cuyler.

With one man out in the third inning, the Cubs' Norman McMillan singled and the next batter, Woody English, doubled. Now the Cubs had runners on second and third with only one out. Rogers Hornsby and Hack Wilson were next in the batting order. Between them, Hornsby and Wilson had hit seventy-nine home runs during the season.

Now Ehmke's scouting efforts produced results. Pitching carefully to their weaknesses, he struck out both Hornsby and Wilson and brought the third inning to a stirring close.

Ehmke reached his peak in the sixth inning. There was still no score and the heart of the Chicago batting order was coming up again: English, Hornsby and Wilson.

Ehmke struck out all three of them, and as they went down, the Chicago spirit went down with them.

But the game was still not won. Although Ehmke was holding off the Cubs, the Athletics weren't having any success against the Chicago pitcher, Charlie Root. Finally, in the seventh inning, Jimmy Foxx, the Athletics' powerful first baseman, lifted a home run into the centerfield bleachers to give Ehmke a 1–0 lead.

The Athletics gave Ehmke two more runs in the ninth inning when right fielder Bing Miller singled with men on second and third. Going into the last of the ninth, Philadelphia was ahead, 3–0.

The Cubs threatened in their last time at bat, with the help of an error by the A's third baseman, Jimmy Dykes. With one out, Kiki Cuyler made it to second base when Dykes fumbled a grounder and then threw wild to first base. The next batter singled and Cuyler came home, making the score 3–1.

First baseman Charley Grimm followed with another single. With one out and the tying run on first base, the Cubs sent up two pinch hitters in a row. But Ehmke rose to the occasion once again and retired them both. He completed his great performance by

striking out the last batter, Charlie Tolson, with runners on first and third.

It was Ehmke's thirteenth strikeout of the game. The pitcher that Connie Mack almost released before the season was over not only beat the Cubs, but he also set a World Series record for strikeouts in one game. Although he never won another major league game, Howard Ehmke had proved that there was "one more good game left in this arm of mine."

mke justified Mr. Mack's gamble by beating one of the hardest-hitting ums ever fielded in a World Series.

16

Opening the Door to Hollywood

A tall, blond young man with a lean frame and a long jaw burst through the door of Branch Rickey's office. Without the usual show of respect, he stalked directly to the old gentleman's desk. The young man leaned over, anger written on his face, and said:

"Don't say a word, Mr. Rickey. This is one conversation I'm conducting."

And in the next ten minutes, Chuck Connors almost talked himself out of the biggest break he would ever get.

The year was 1950. Rickey was then general manager of the Brooklyn Dodgers. The scene was Vero Beach, Florida, where the Dodgers were in spring training. Connors was a first baseman who had been a member of the Dodger organization since 1942.

Before signing with the Dodgers, Connors had attended Seton Hall College where he excelled in public speaking as well as sports. Not only was he a baseball player, but he had done well enough in basketball at Seton Hall to get a chance with the Boston Celtics of the National Basketball Association. However, baseball was his game, and he had moved up gradually through the farm system to the Dodgers.

He was getting his second chance with the Dodgers in 1950 when he confronted Rickey. Connors was known as quite a "ham" among the ballplayers, and he was strictly on-stage with Rickey. His speech was

Chuck practices his slide during spring training at the Dodger camp in 1949.

well-planned, complete with dramatic gestures and dramatic pauses.

Connors reminded Rickey that he had been a star at Montreal the year before, batting .319. Such a performance entitled him to a chance to play regularly with the Dodgers, he said. His conclusion may have been intended as a threat. He told Rickey that if he weren't given a chance with the Dodgers, he wanted to be traded to a team where he could play regularly.

Rickey did not interrupt the rookie's intense presentation. He had known of Connors chiefly through his clubhouse antics. Connors had kept his teammates entertained with his renditions of "Casey at the Bat" and his tricks of magic. He had a flexible face and mimicry came easy for him. One night in a camp show at Vero Beach, Connors had gained the spotlight with an imitation of Rickey himself, picturing Rickey as a merciless penny pincher and the Dodger camp as a prison.

Although Connors had tried everything to get a chance at first base, Manager Shotton had persistently stuck to Gil Hodges and Dee Fondy. Occasionally he would call on Connors, but usually he appeared only in "B" squad games. Rickey may have recalled, as he watched Connors' dramatics, that Connors had been to bat only once in the National League and had hit into a double play.

"My boy," said Rickey, as Connors finished, "you are absolutely right. You deserve the chance to play more often. I'll give it to you right now."

In the time that it takes to place a long distance telephone call, Rickey sold Connors to the St. Louis Browns. Connors was crestfallen. This was worse than being in Montreal, because the Browns were the worst club in the American League. Besides, they paid even lower salaries than the Dodgers.

Two hours later, after he had wandered about the camp thinking about what he had done, Connors was back at Rickey's door again.

"Call it off, Mr. Rickey, please," he said. "I'll go to Montreal, if you promise to trade me to another National League club at the end of the season."

Rickey agreed, and at the end of the season Connors was sold to the Chicago Cubs. Even with this lowly member of the National League he couldn't break into the line-up. Shortly afterward he found himself playing on option in Los Angeles with a Pacific Coast League team. To add to his discouragement, Connors had been beaten out in Chicago by one of his Brooklyn teammates who had also been traded to the Cubs, Dee Fondy.

It was a despondent Connors who reported to Los Angeles at the beginning of the 1951 season. What he didn't know was that he was walking into an opportunity that would completely reshape his life.

Movie figures are devoted baseball fans in Los Angeles. They were attracted to Connors, who had now carried his antics to the playing field. He was also hitting home runs with impressive regularity, and this made him even more noticeable.

In fact, his fine performance even brought about the one big baseball break he had been playing for. At midseason, he had a batting average of .321, with 22 home runs and 77 runs batted in, and the Cubs recalled him.

Connors finished the season in Chicago, but he was a big disappointment to himself and to the Cubs. After batting only .239 in 66 games, he was returned to Los Angeles for the 1952 season. He increased his mischievousness on the field. "If I'm not going to make it in the big leagues," he told a teammate, "I might as well have some fun out of life."

One night Connors hit a home run, and as he neared second on his way around the bases, he suddenly slid into the bag in a cloud of dust, and arose making a sweeping bow. When he reached the plate, he stopped and vigorously shook the hand of the opposing catcher, then hammed it up all the way back to the dugout.

After the game, there was a call for Connors at the Angels' dressing room: a man named Grady from MGM. Connors was somewhat suspicious, but went out to meet the man anyway. The caller was Bill

Grady, a casting director from Metro–Goldwyn–Mayer, one of Hollywood's biggest movie studios. He offered Connors the chance to make $500 a day as an actor. Connors could hardly believe his ears.

As it turned out, Chuck didn't get the part that Grady had picked him for, a prize-fight tough. Connors just couldn't look battered enough or dumb enough for the role. But he did get the part of a clean-cut state patrolman.

After receiving his check for $500, he called Bill Grady. "Any more jobs like that around?" Chuck asked.

"Not right now," Grady told him, "but I'll keep you in mind."

Shortly afterward Connors did get a call from Grady. "I've got a part for you in 'South Seas Woman,'" he said.

This paid $750 a week, and the job lasted thirteen weeks. Altogether during that winter, Chuck made $15,000 as a movie actor. He had made only $6,500 in his eighth season as a baseball player the previous summer.

When Connors' baseball contract arrived, it was another invitation to join the Cubs. He had developed a big following among Los Angeles fans and the Cubs wanted him back. Despite this second chance with the Chicago team, baseball had become less important to Connors. He decided to quit baseball altogether. Chuck Connors, first baseman, became Chuck Connors, actor.

His reputation grew rapidly in Hollywood. He received many movie parts, usually in Westerns. Then, television called and his audience grew. He played the title role in the "The Rifleman" series. Next, he starred in "Branded" and then organized his own production company.

Although his career as a first baseman never worked out the way he planned it, Chuck never failed to be grateful to baseball for opening the door to Hollywood.

In his first season as an actor Chuck Connors earned more than twice his salary as a baseball player. He is seen here as the hero of the TV show "Branded."

17
The Shoeshine Pitch

The fourth game of the 1957 World Series is described by many baseball observers as one of the most exciting in history. Had it not been for Vernal "Nippy" Jones, it might not have been.

The Milwaukee Braves were playing their first World Series since the team had been moved from Boston. The Series had opened in New York, where the Braves lost the first game to the Yankees and won the second.

Wisconsin was bursting with excitement when the two teams moved to Milwaukee for the next three games. It was the first time a World Series had ever been played in Wisconsin. Some of the enthusiasm faded, however, when the Braves' pitchers walked eleven Yankees and lost the first home game, 12–3.

Going into the fourth game, the Braves were trailing, two games to one. Warren Spahn, the greatest left-handed pitcher in baseball, was chosen to pitch against the Yankees. The appearance of their pitching star restored confidence to the anxious Milwaukeeans.

After eight innings, the crafty veteran led the Yankees by a score of 4–1. He retired the first two batters in the ninth, but then Yogi Berra, the squat Yankee catcher, singled. So did the next batter, Gil McDougald.

Apprehension spread among loyal Braves fans, but

With a 3 and 2 count on Elston Howard, Spahn gave up a three-run homer which tied the fourth game of the 1957 Series.

many thousands of them who had made an early start to the parking lot kept moving. Surely Spahn would not let them down this close to victory. A conference was held on the mound. Manager Fred Haney was confident, too, that Spahn would not let the Braves down. He offered a few words of encouragement and went back to the dugout, leaving the crisis in Spahn's care.

Elston Howard was the next Yankee at bat. He was a dangerous right-handed hitter. Spahn worked carefully and the count reached 3 and 2.

"This is it," said the radio announcer. "The Yankees trail 4–1 in the top of the ninth. There are two out and two men on. The count on Elston Howard is three balls, two strikes. . . .

"Spahn sets, checks both runners and delivers. Howard swings and he gets hold of one . . . It's a long fly . . . it's going, going . . ."

There was no doubt about it—it was a home run. With one swing of the bat, Elston Howard had tied the game. In the parking lot, there was confusion. Milwaukee fans gulped. Many rushed back to their seats in the stadium. Others tuned in the game on their automobile radios and hoped. This couldn't happen, they thought. The Yankees couldn't win. If they beat Spahn, the Braves' ace, the World Series was lost.

Milwaukee failed to score in the ninth, and the tenth began on an ominous note. Tony Kubek of the Yankees, a native Milwaukeean, beat out an infield roller. Hank Bauer then hit a triple that scored Kubek and put New York in the lead, 5–4.

Defeat seemed certain as the Braves came to bat in the tenth inning. There was little cause for rejoicing when it was announced that number 25, Nippy Jones, would bat for Spahn.

Jones was what is known in professional baseball

as a "retread," meaning that he had played in the major leagues and then had been sent back to the minors. He had been the regular first baseman for the Cardinals at one time and later played for the Phillies. An injury to his back followed by a serious operation brought an end to his usefulness as a day-by-day player and his release to the minors.

When Joe Adcock, the Braves' star first baseman, suffered a broken leg in midseason, Jones was hastily brought up to Milwaukee from Sacramento, a Pacific Coast League team. Jones had been used chiefly as a relief player during the season, filling in at first base on occasion, and pinch-hitting.

Now he walked to the plate, a slight, somber man with dark, sad eyes. He tapped the dirt from his spikes, and faced Tommy Byrne, a Yankee relief pitcher known for his wildness.

Byrne's first pitch was low. The ball got away from catcher Yogi Berra and skittered back to the grandstand wall. Jones started toward first base, but was called back by umpire Augie Donatelli. A fierce argument broke out. Jones argued that the pitch had hit his foot. Donatelli said the pitch was a ball and ordered Jones back into the batter's box.

As the argument raged, the ball rolled back on the rebound from the cement wall, coming to rest between Jones and Donatelli. The crowd saw Jones reach

Ump Augie Donatelli shows game-winning shoe polish to catcher Yogi Berra while Nippy Jones points to his shoes. The Braves went on to win the Series in seven games.

suddenly for the ball, then thrust it in the face of Donatelli.

"Here!" Jones cried, "Look at the shoe polish on the ball!"

There was a black splotch on the baseball, and as Jones pointed first to the ball, then to his brightly shined shoes, Donatelli was convinced. The Milwaukee pinch hitter was awarded first base. He was immediately replaced by a pinch runner. He retired to the dugout and did not appear again in the series.

But this insignificant incident seemed to set the Braves on fire. Their shortstop, Johnny Logan, slashed a double into left field, scoring the pinch runner and tying the game. Casey Stengel came out to change pitchers and the Milwaukee fans jeered the crusty old Yankee manager.

Ed Mathews, the Braves' power-hitting third baseman, came up to face the new pitcher, Bob Grim. Mathews looked at a couple of pitches, then swung on a fast ball and drove a home run into the right center field bleachers, scoring Logan ahead of him, and winning the game, 7–5.

Milwaukee went wild that night. The fans had seen the Yankees beaten and the Series tied at two games apiece. Encouraged by their victory, the Braves rode on to triumph in seven games. Lou Burdette, a rawboned, right-handed pitcher, won three games, and Henry Aaron, the center fielder, was the batting leader.

But the great Braves victory might never have happened if it hadn't been for Nippy Jones, who kept his shoes well shined.

18
Back Road to the Hall of Fame

Dazzy Vance was never sure what happened to his pitching arm early in his career. He thought he injured it for the first time boxing with one of his brothers before he left his home near Red Cloud, Nebraska, for spring training in 1916. He was hoping to join the New York Yankees, for whom he had pitched in nine games the season before without a victory.

He was sent to the minors for the 1916 season and for the next five years his pitching career was hampered by his sore arm. Managers began to squint at him suspiciously and ask, "Vance, do you really *want* to pitch, or not?"

Sometimes Vance felt like telling them the truth. His arm often hurt so badly that he really *didn't* want to pitch. But he had a family to support and baseball was the only business he knew.

Once, when he was pitching for Columbus, Ohio, he stuck his elbow in ice water between innings to numb the pain. This worked for a couple of games. Finally even the ice water did no good, and the Columbus club sent him home to see a doctor in Nebraska.

"I can't tell you exactly what the trouble is," the doctor told Vance, "but I believe that if you can keep from hurting it again in the next four or five years, it'll come around all right."

"Four to five years, Doc!" Vance exclaimed. "And how am I going to eat in the meantime?"

In the spring of 1917 Vance was back in training, this time with the Toledo, Ohio, team. He looked great in exhibitions, but as the season opened he began to tire easily and the opposition started to slaughter him. He moved on to Memphis but the same thing happened. At first Vance dazzled batters with his fiery fast ball, but then he would tire and have to leave the game. He was called up to the New York Yankees again in 1918. But he pitched only two games before returning to the minors.

This was the pattern of Dazzy Vance's life until 1920, when he found himself in Memphis. The manager of the Memphis team was a grumpy veteran named Spencer Abbott. Short of patience and firmly convinced that Vance was too lazy or too yellow to pitch, he traded the tall right-hander to New Orleans.

Soon Vance's arm was beginning to feel good again. About two weeks after being traded to New Orleans, Vance beat Memphis with a terrific performance. Abbott was angry. "Why didn't you pitch that way for me?" he said to Vance, meeting him in the hotel doorway that night.

"I kept trying to tell you," Vance said. "I didn't have my strength yet, and I needed plenty of rest. They're giving me rest at New Orleans, and I'm winning."

Vance kept on winning. The next season at New Orleans—1921—he won twenty-one games. This attracted the attention of the Brooklyn Dodgers, but only by accident.

New Orleans had a catcher named Hank DeBerry who was making a name for himself in the Southern Association. Wilbert Robinson, manager of the Dodgers, needed a catcher badly and sent his top scout, Larry Sutton, to take a look at DeBarry.

Returning to Brooklyn, Sutton told Robinson, "We not only need DeBerry, but they've got a pitcher we ought to get, too. His name is Vance."

By this time Vance was thirty-one years old, though nobody but his family knew it. He had played with twelve different teams in every kind of town, and his sore arm was well-known. Nevertheless, Sutton insisted that Robinson buy him. And Vance became a Dodger.

Not many people were optimistic about Vance's chance of staying with the National League team. Even Vance wondered if he could make it. But, one day in Mobile, Alabama, the Dodgers stopped to play the St. Louis Browns in a spring exhibition game. George Sisler, one of the great hitters of all time, came to bat against Vance. The 31-year-old rookie reared back in a big sweeping motion until his arm almost touched the ground, then delivered the ball with a big kick of the foot. It was a strike.

With two strikes on Sisler, Vance broke off a big curve that caught the great hitter with his bat on the shoulder. Sisler knew he was out, and he turned and walked away without a word.

"They told me Vance was strictly a fast-ball pitcher," Robinson said, excitedly. "Look at the way he got Sisler on that curve. Anybody who can catch Sisler looking at a curve must be throwing a pretty good one."

From then on, Vance was established as a Dodger. He won eighteen games during his first season and led the league in strikeouts. He won eighteen games the next year and again led the league in strikeouts. His third season with the Dodgers was his finest. He won twenty-eight games and lost only six. Once again he led the league in strikeouts, and he was voted the most valuable player. Vance led in strikeouts seven years in a row, something no other pitcher has ever done.

His name became synonymous with speed. Little boys playing sandlot ball and fancying themselves as hitters pretended they were Babe Ruth. Sandlot pitchers who tried to throw the ball hard were patterning themselves after Dazzy Vance.

When he retired, Vance had won 197 games and

Dazzy was traded to New Orleans because his manager thought he was too lazy or too yellow to pitch.

had struck out 2,045 batters. He pitched until he was forty-four years old, and in the twilight of his career realized one of his cherished ambitions. In 1934 he made his only appearance in a World Series, pitching in relief for the St. Louis Cardinals against Detroit. He pitched only one and one-third innings, but he was at his dazzling best, shutting out the Tigers and striking out three batters.

Vance's last great thrill came to him many years later, a most improbable climax to a most improbable career. One spring day in 1954, as he drove along a highway near his home in Homosassa Springs, Florida, a state patrolman roared up behind him and motioned him over to the side of the road.

"Hey, what's the big idea?" asked Dazzy as the patrolman approached his car. "Is something wrong?"

"Not a thing, Mr. Vance," said the patrolman. "Everything's fine, in fact. I just stopped you to tell you that you've been voted into the Hall of Fame."

What are the odds against a pitcher who didn't win his first game in the major leagues until he was thirty-one years old ever making the Baseball Hall of Fame? Maybe 1,000,000 to 1. But Dazzy Vance made it and he did it the hard way, sore arm and all.

s a Dodger, Vance became a sandlot idol. His name was synonymous ith a blazing fastball.

19

Lt. Shepard of the Big Leagues

One day in early March, 1945, a young man named Bert Shepard appeared at the preseason training camp of the Washington Senators at College Park, Maryland, and sought out Manager Ossie Bluege.

"I'd like to get a tryout, Mr. Bluege," the young man said.

Bluege, a man with cold, steel-blue eyes, looked the applicant up and down. "What experience have you had?" he asked.

Shepard explained that he had played in the Wisconsin State League, the Evangeline League and the Arizona-Texas League. During the war, he said, he had pitched and played first base for service teams.

The United States was still at war with the Germans and the Japanese. Baseball players were becoming more scarce each day, since nearly all able-bodied men were in the armed forces. No sensible manager would turn down any likely applicant, especially one who looked as healthy and athletic as this one. Bluege took Shepard to the clubhouse and asked the trainer to find a uniform for him.

The day's workout hadn't yet begun. A few Washington players still loitered in the clubhouse as Shepard began to change from street clothes into the flannel uniform. At first, the other players didn't take much notice of him. In those times they were accustomed to seeing players walk in off the street, ask for a tryout and just as suddenly disappear.

But as Bert Shepard switched trousers, it was easy to see that he had an artificial leg. He was a one-legged player.

When he walked onto the field his limp was noticeable, but only because the other players now knew of his handicap. They were amazed and touched to see a one-legged man who insisted he could play professional baseball. He soon proved that he could.

Being a professional baseball player was Bert Shepard's big ambition when he enlisted in the Army in 1942. Now the war was over for him but his ambition was still the same.

The baseball season was supposed to begin for the 55th Fighter Group team, based in England, on May 21, 1944. Lieutenant Bert Shepard was the manager as well as the star pitcher. First, though, there was a mission to be flown over Germany.

Early that morning, Lieutenant Shepard and a flight of P-38 fighter planes set out for the target in Germany. By this time Shepard was a veteran. He had flown thirty-three missions, and he felt that he was the master of the sky.

The game was scheduled for 2 P.M. There was plenty of time to complete the mission and get back to play, he thought, as he flew over the North Sea toward the target at 300 miles per hour.

The attacking force had completed its run on the target and was preparing to head back to base when Shepard spotted a train chugging along below. One purpose of the mission was to strafe anything that moved, and Lieutenant Shepard put his P-38 into a dive toward the train. The train was in smoke and flames, and he was about to pull up when ground fire struck the cockpit. He tried desperately to pull out of range, but then another burst of fire hit him. That is the last he remembered.

Several days later, he awoke in a German prison hospital and discovered that his right leg was missing, amputated just below the knee. It had been mangled by antiaircraft fire, and the German doctors had hurriedly removed it. They had done a good job, but what use is a one-legged baseball player?

The longer he lay in bed, however, the more determined he became that he should be a baseball player, even with only one leg. Meanwhile, back at the 55th Fighter Group base in England, the boys on the baseball team finally gave up hope for their manager after two weeks.

Shepard had been in the Washington Senators' camp only five days when newsreel cameramen appeared to make movies of this unusual baseball player.

It would be great for the soldiers' morale.

"Can you field bunts?" one of them asked.

Shepard had been wearing his artificial leg only one week. It had been attached the day before he left nearby Walter Reed Hospital. But he was game. "Sure, I can field bunts," he said. "Let me know when you're ready."

Al Evans stepped up to bat. Shepard pitched and Evans laid the ball down between the mound and third base. Shepard swooped down on it, wheeled as a left-handed pitcher must and threw Evans out by a step.

On April first, the Senators traveled to Norfolk, Virginia, to play the Naval Training base team. With a comfortable lead in the eighth inning, Bluege decided to test the one-legged pitcher and Shepard marched to the mound with 8,000 servicemen looking on.

The first batter immediately laid down a bunt. Shepard whipped off the mound, pounced on the ball and threw the runner out easily, while servicemen cheered in approval. The next batter grounded out to first and the second hit a fly to center field.

That was enough. Shepard had proved he could pitch, run and even pinch-hit, if necessary. Clark Griffith, the white-haired owner of the Senators, signed him to a contract. There was never a happier

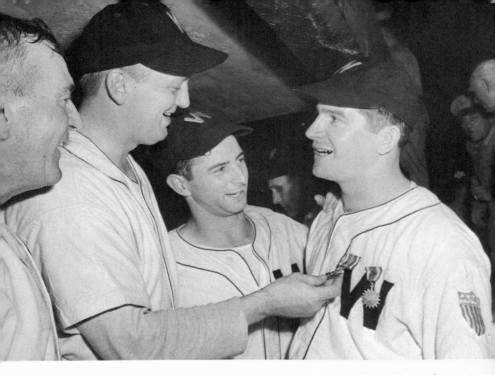

Teammates admire the Distinguished Flying Cross awarded to Shepard during a colorful homeplate ceremony.

man than Bert Shepard.

The first few weeks of the 1945 season weren't easy for him. He wanted to pitch, but Bluege used him mostly for batting practice, and Griffith used him mostly as a display to other handicapped servicemen who might be feeling sorry for themselves. Frequently Shepard went back to his old ward at Walter Reed Hospital to cheer up his wounded comrades.

Finally, one day in July, he got his first real chance. The Senators were scheduled to play the Brooklyn Dodgers in a war-relief exhibition game.

Bluege asked Shepard if he thought he could beat

them. Shepard, knowing that this was his first chance against major league competition, said he thought he could. Bluege started him in the exhibition. Shepard pitched against the Dodgers and was credited with the victory.

Late in July, the Senators were playing Boston and found themselves several runs behind early in the game. Bluege saw that he would need a relief pitcher to start the next inning and told Shepard to warm up. But the Red Sox kept up a steady bombardment and finally Bluege had to come out of the dugout.

After a conference with the pitcher, he motioned for Shepard. The former fighter pilot, walking with that slight trace of a limp, moved from the bull pen to the pitcher's mound. Everybody knew of him by now, and his performance was watched intently.

Shepard retired the last man of the inning. Then he went one, two, three innings. Finally the Red Sox got a run, but he finished the fifth relief inning and the game. Boston had managed to get only three hits and one run in the five innings and he had struck out three batters.

Shepard's career was a short one. His leg was bothering him. He had to return to Walter Reed Hospital for adjustments of the artificial limb. Afterward, the Senators sent him to their Chattanooga farm

Even with a wooden leg, Bert could pitch, run and hit. Here he warms up for the Washington Senators.

team, where he won two games and lost two games.

"I'll be back," he said when he left.

He did return to the Senators, but they never used him in another regular season game. Still, he had kept the vow he made in a hospital bed in Germany. Bert Shepard had become a major league pitcher, if only for a day.

20
The Tag-Along

When they were kids in Phoenix, Arizona, Ted Smith wanted to be a big league baseball player and Gordon Windhorn dreamed of nothing but being a track star. Whenever there was a baseball game in the neighborhood, Ted would show up with his glove in his hand. Gordon was a good runner and concentrated on making his high-school track team.

One day a notice appeared in a Phoenix newspaper that the New York Giants would conduct a baseball tryout in the city. Ted had played sandlot baseball and his coaches had told him he was a good outfielder. A tryout with the New York Giants, he felt, was his big chance.

There was just one drawback. Ted was shy and didn't want to go alone. Gordon Windhorn was his good friend, so Ted decided to ask him to go to the tryouts. Gordon had played baseball only a few times. When Ted asked him to go along, he protested that he didn't even have any equipment. Ted offered to borrow some for him and Gordon reluctantly agreed to go.

The next afternoon, Ted went to the Windhorn home carrying a baseball uniform, a glove and spikes for Gordon and a set of equipment for himself. Arriving at the ball park, the two boys were sent to a locker room to dress.

"I feel silly, putting this thing on," Gordon said,

buttoning his baseball shirt. "I'm a runner, not a baseball player."

"Baseball players have to run, too," Ted said. "Tell
them you're an outfielder. All they'll do is hit fly balls
to you and you can catch them easily."

Despite Ted's assurances, Gordon was afraid of
making a fool of himself. Out on the field, he took
his glove and eased toward the outfield, hoping
nobody would notice him.

"Hey, boy!" shouted a uniformed man with a bat.
"Get this one!"

The man lofted a fly over Gordon's head. Gordon
turned in two directions, then set out on a run. He
stuck out his glove and the ball hit it with a plop—
a perfect catch! The man hit another, and once again
Gordon managed to get under the ball and catch it.
There was something lacking in his style, but with
great bursts of speed he always managed to get to
the ball.

A little later, Gordon was called in to the dugout.
"You're the kid that was making all those catches out
there, aren't you?" said the man in charge. "Now
let's see what you can do with a bat."

Gordon said, "Okay, mister, I'll try." He had played
softball a few times and he knew at least how to
swing a bat.

Gordon rifled the first pitch to left field for a clean

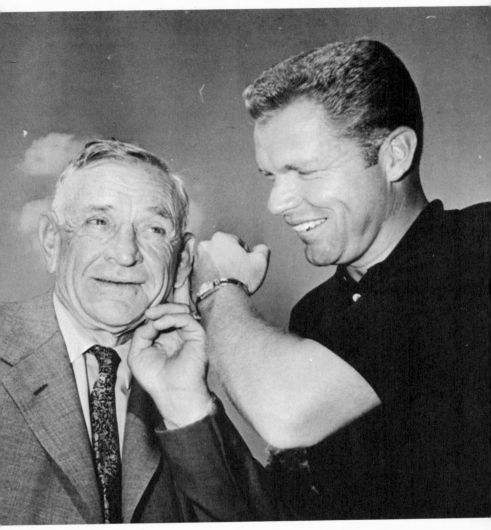

Outfielder Windhorn shows Yankee manager Casey Stengel the wrist watch awarded to him as outstanding Yankee rookie.

hit. He hit the next one so hard that Ted, who had been moved in to shortstop, couldn't handle it. This impressive exhibition continued through five more pitches, after which Gordon was allowed to return to the outfield.

When the tryout was over that afternoon, the uniformed man called all the players around him. He picked out five and asked them to step to one side. One of them was Gordon Windhorn.

"How would you boys like to play for the New York Giants?" he said. "If you would, I've got contracts here for all of you."

In the crowd of players who didn't make it, Gordon could see the crestfallen face of his friend, Ted Smith. He could hardly force himself to look at Ted as they walked home.

"Honest, Ted, I never had any idea I could play baseball," he said. "I'm awful sorry."

"Sorry?" Ted said. "It's great. It won't be long. I'll make it sometime, too, and we'll play in the big leagues together."

But Ted never made it. He finally gave up the game and found a job in Phoenix. Gordon Windhorn was never a big star, but he did play for the Red Sox, the Yankees, the Kansas City Athletics and the Los Angeles Dodgers. He is one of the few who became a major league player by accident.

Playing for the Los Angeles Dodgers, Windhorn slams into the wall in an effort to catch a long fly.

21
Young Man in a Hurry

Ty Cobb's father was a stern man who took a dim view of his son's interest in professional baseball. He was a superintendent of schools in Royston, Georgia, and he regarded baseball as a game for boys and men who were too lazy to get a steady job. But since his son was determined to try out for the minor league team in Augusta, Georgia, Mr. Cobb thought it best to let young Ty get baseball out of his system. He gave Ty 90 dollars and several letters of introduction to people who might help him if his baseball career didn't work out. Then he sent him on his way.

Two days after the baseball season opened in Augusta, Ty, who was only seventeen years old, suddenly found himself out of work. The manager of the Augusta team, a grumpy man named Con Strouthers, called him in and gave him his release.

Another player, released at the same time, had an offer from a semiprofessional team in Anniston, Alabama, and invited Cobb to join him. Ty wanted to go along but decided to call his father first. It was a nervous young man who telephoned from Augusta to Royston that night, explaining to his father that he had been released from the Augusta team and asking permission to try his luck in Alabama. There was a long pause while the static cracked over the telephone lines. Then Mr. Cobb spoke. "Go after it," he said, "and don't come.home a failure."

The Anniston team was made up mostly of young collegians and a few wandering ex-professionals. The club paid Cobb 65 dollars a month, plus room and board in a private home. After Augusta, making the Anniston team was easy. Soon, Cobb became one of the best hitters in the league. But since this was a semiprofessional league, little news of his success got beyond the local papers. None of it got as far as the Atlanta *Journal*, which his father subscribed to and read every day.

One day, Grantland Rice, the popular young sports editor of the *Journal*, received a post card from Anniston, telling him about the splendid young outfielder named Cobb:

Ty Cobb, dashing young star with Anniston, Alabama, is going great guns. He is as fast as a deer and undoubtedly a phenom.
(Signed) Mr. Jones

Soon another card reached Rice's desk. It said:

Cobb had three hits yesterday, made two sensational catches. Keep your eye on this phenom.
(Signed) Smith, Brown, Kelly and McIntyre

More cards and letters arrived, all recommending this superb young outfielder from Anniston:

oung Ty Cobb was hardly modest but who could object? He had a
tting average of .370!

If you're searching for a future star, he's playing here in Anniston. His name is Cobb. He's a Georgia boy who's going a long way.

(Signed) Interested Fan

This is the one that aroused Rice's writing interest. Since this fantastic lad with the enthusiastic backing was a Georgia boy, he should be mentioned in Rice's column.

He finally wrote one day, "Rumors have reached Atlanta from numerous sources that over in Alabama there's a young fellow named Cobb who seems to be showing an unusual lot of talent for baseball. Furthermore, he's a Georgian."

Back in Royston, Mr. Cobb clipped the little article out of the *Journal* and carried it in his wallet as proof that his son had made good. And in Augusta, the article encouraged the baseball team to do some checking. It soon learned that the slender young man who had been hastily dismissed was batting .370 in Anniston. He was soon brought back and restored to the line-up.

There was no slowing Cobb's drive to the top now. He finished the 1904 season with Augusta and was called to the Detroit Tigers before the next season was over. There he became one of the truly great baseball players. He never did get baseball out of

It was many years before sports writer Grantland Rice learned who had written all those glowing reports on Cobb.

his system as his father had hoped. He played for twenty-four years in the major leagues. After his first season, he never batted below .300 and he led the American League in batting eleven times. Three times he batted over .400. In addition, he stole 892 bases. Years later, he was one of the first five men voted into the Baseball Hall of Fame. He received more votes than Babe Ruth or Christy Mathewson.

Many years later, Cobb happened to be seated next to Grantland Rice on the speaker's platform at a sports banquet. Cobb was nearing the end of his great playing career with Detroit and Rice had been successful, too; he had become the most famous sports writer in America.

The speakers were reminiscing about great past sports events and when Cobb's turn came, he spoke to Rice. "Grant," he began, "you remember when you were sports editor of the Atlanta *Journal,* and I was just starting out in baseball?"

"You bet I remember," Rice said. "I first heard of you when you were playing for a team in Anniston, Alabama."

"And do you remember all the cards and letters you used to get from the fans in Anniston, telling you what a great prospect I was?" Cobb asked.

"They swamped me," Rice said. "In fact, they wrote you right out of Anniston back to Augusta."

"I was playing pretty well," Cobb said, "but I must have been a pretty good writer, too, because I wrote those cards and letters myself."

Rice was silent for a moment. The joke was certainly on him. But then his face broke into a big smile. He reached out and shook Cobb's hand, and they both understood.

Cobb would have succeeded in baseball sooner or later. He had too much talent to be ignored for long. But even when he was only seventeen, he had a tremendous desire to succeed—he had been a young man in a big hurry.

22

Two for the Price of One

A crowd of only 3,500 came out to Weeghman Park in Chicago on the afternoon of May 2, 1917. Weeghman Park, the home of the Chicago Cubs, was later renamed Wrigley Field. It was a weekday, accounting for the light attendance, and the Cubs were playing the Cincinnati Reds. If Cub fans had known what was going to happen they would have come in greater numbers.

Jim "Hippo" Vaughn, a big left-handed pitcher from Texas, was starting for the Cubs against Cincinnati's Fred Toney, a right-hander from Tennessee. Both pitchers were on their way to splendid seasons, Toney to win 24 games and Vaughn to win 23.

Something extra rode on the game because Toney and Vaughn were not particularly friendly. Vaughn came from a tough breed of players who felt that even to speak to a member of another team on the field violated an unwritten code.

The first inning began with two Cincinnati batters going down in rapid order. The third Red, outfielder Earle "Greasy" Neale (he was later head football coach of the Philadelphia Eagles) hit a soft line drive that looked like a hit. But the Cubs' right fielder, Cy Williams, put on a burst of speed coming in for the ball, and made the catch at his shoetops. Otherwise, the game moved along without any threat of a hit for several innings.

153

Reds Manager Pat Moran had stacked the Cincinnati line-up with right-handed hitters, since the averages said that right-handers would be more likely to hit Vaughn's left-handed pitching. This had been no handicap to Vaughn, however. He had been mowing down the Reds with regularity.

After he had set down Cincinnati in the eighth inning, Vaughn reached the bench in time to hear a teammate say, "Come on, fellows, let's get a run off this guy!"

"Get a run?" said another Cub. "Somebody better think about getting a hit first."

"Well," said the first teammate, "they haven't got a hit off Hippo yet, either."

Suddenly Vaughn realized that both he and Toney had no-hit games within their reach. As he silently pulled on his sweater to keep his arm warm between innings, Vaughn thought to himself, "Well, if this is a no-hitter and there's only one more inning to go, I'm going to give it all I've got."

Once again in the last of the eighth the Cubs went up to bat and down in one–two–three order, and Vaughn headed back to the mound for the ninth inning. The first man up hit a line drive to the Cub third baseman. Vaughn threw three strikes past Emil Huhn, the weak-hitting Cincinnati catcher.

That brought up Toney, a big man and a dangerous

hitter for a pitcher. He had a powerful stiff-armed swing, and on Vaughn's first pitch he swung fiercely and missed. Two more pitches, each a fast ball, put Toney out on strikes to end the inning, but it was a tired Vaughn who returned to the Chicago dugout.

In the last of the ninth Toney set down the Cubs in order again. This was enough for historical purposes. Both pitchers had pitched complete no-hit games against one another, the only time it has ever happened in the major leagues.

But the game still had to be won. The small crowd sounded like 10,000 as they cheered Vaughn on his weary way back to the mound to face the Reds in the first half of the tenth inning.

Gus Getz, the first Red to bat, popped out to catcher Art Wilson. The next batter, shortstop Larry Kopf, was only a .255 batter, but he broke the spell. He slapped a ground ball between the first and second baseman into right field for the first hit of the game. Vaughn then retired Neale on a fly ball to Williams, and it looked as though he was out of trouble, even though his no-hitter was gone.

But then misfortune fell on the Cubs. Hal Chase, the Cincinnati first baseman, hit a sinking line drive to center field. Williams reached the ball in time for the catch—but he dropped it for an error. Now Kopf was on third, Chase was on first, and Indian Jim

Thorpe was at bat.

Although Thorpe excelled as a college football player and as an Olympic track star, he never mastered baseball. He was swift as a deer and had a strong arm, but his downfall was the curve ball. He could hit a fast ball out of the park, but throw him a curve and he was helpless. Jim had already struck out twice that afternoon on Vaughn's curve.

As Vaughn delivered his first pitch, Chase broke for second and slid in with a clean steal. Vaughn worked very carefully on Thorpe. With two runners in scoring position, naturally he called on his curve and Thorpe swung, topping the ball and sending it spinning down the third baseline.

Big Vaughn leaped from the mound and fielded the ball, but too late to make a play for the speedy Thorpe at first. Had he not had his back to Kopf, he could have turned and tagged the Cincinnati shortstop. But Kopf sped by him and headed for the plate.

There was still time to get Kopf at home, and Vaughn threw to Wilson, the catcher. For some reason, Wilson was looking toward first base, apparently expecting the play there. The ball hit his chest protector and dropped to the ground while Kopf slid under him. Now Chase was also on his way toward the plate. Wilson, coming out of his stupor, scrambled for the third out.

The damage was done, though. The Reds were ahead 1–0 and Toney again retired the Cubs in order in the last of the tenth. The double no-hitter was over, Toney the winner, Vaughn the loser.

In the clubhouse, Wilson was in tears. "I just passed out on you Jim," he said to Vaughn. "I just passed out. It was all my fault."

Vaughn was a good sport, however. "Don't blame yourself, Art," he told his catcher. "It's just another ball game."

It was hardly just another ball game. There has never been one like it in the major leagues. Because of his defeat that day, Jim Vaughn promised himself he would never lose again to Fred Toney. And he never did.

23

The
Iron
Horse

On June 2, 1925, the first baseman for the New York Yankees, a veteran named Wally Pipp, told Manager Miller Huggins that he had a headache and would appreciate the day off. Huggins was sympathetic and decided to give the "new kid" a chance.

The "new kid" was Lou Gehrig who had not yet reached his twenty-second birthday. He had been discovered two years earlier when he was a pitcher and outfielder for Columbia University and had played in only a handful of games for the Yankees. But as Pipp said later, what he got that day wasn't a rest, it was a retirement. Young Gehrig did so well at first base that Pipp never got back into the regular line-up and was sold the next season to Cincinnati.

It was nearly fourteen years before Gehrig gave up his place in the line-up. Starting on June 2, 1925, he played in every Yankee game until May 1, 1939. He appeared in 2,130 consecutive games, a record so amazing that it is likely never to be broken. For his reliability, Gehrig was called "The Iron Horse."

But Gehrig was more than reliable. As a young man of twenty-two, he had earned a place with the New York Yankees, who were then the strongest team in baseball. One of Gehrig's teammates was Babe Ruth, who had already established himself as the "Home Run King." But even though the Yankees were one of the greatest teams in history, Gehrig soon be-

Lou, shown here fresh out of Columbia University, was soon to become known as "The Iron Horse."

came one of the greatest of the great.

Two years after he took Wally Pipp's place at first base, Gehrig showed his talent. It was 1927. The Yankees won the pennant by nineteen games and Babe Ruth became a baseball legend by hitting sixty home runs. Meanwhile, Gehrig batted .373 and set another all-time record by batting in 175 runs. When the award to the most valuable player in the league was given, it went not to the famous and colorful Ruth but to Lou Gehrig, who was still in his early twenties.

Gehrig went on to break his own RBI record, batting in 184 runs in 1931, a record that still stands in the American League. He led the league five times in runs batted in, four times in runs scored, three times in home runs and once in batting average. Perhaps more important, he was named the most valuable player in his league four times.

As the season ended in 1938, a few fans and writers wondered if Gehrig was beginning to fade. He had batted only .295, the first time his average had fallen under .300 in thirteen seasons. Although he had hit 29 home runs and batted in 114 runs—a good performance for most players—he was still not as sharp as he had been in previous years.

In the spring of 1939, Gehrig was even less impressive. He seemed to move around rather stiffly and his batting eye was off. Sports writers had reported that he was suffering from lumbago during the previous season and many assumed that it was still plaguing him. During the first eight games, Gehrig could get only four hits, all singles. His batting average was .143. In the field, he was clumsy and slow, although people remembered him as a fine first baseman.

On April 30, the Yankees set out on their first

Lou makes a play at first base.

Western trip of the season. Gehrig had played in the last home game against Washington that afternoon and by the time the team reached Detroit he had reached a great personal decision. He came down from his room in the Book Cadillac Hotel and found the Yankee manager, Joe McCarthy, in the lobby. He asked for a private word with him.

"I think you'd better put Babe Dahlgren in at first base today," Gehrig told McCarthy. "I'm not doing myself or the team any good."

McCarthy tried to talk Lou out of his decision but Gehrig stood firm.

"The other day I made a routine play at first base," he said, "and when I got back to the bench the fellows said 'Nice play, Lou.' When they start feeling sorry for you and it shows, it's time to quit."

McCarthy reluctantly called a press conference and announced that "The Iron Horse" was benching himself. This was more than an ordinary change in the line-up. It was the end of Gehrig's great endurance record.

When Gehrig's withdrawal from the line-up was announced, most people assumed that it would mean only a short rest, because he was only thirty-five. But like Wally Pipp, who had given up his place for a rest fourteen years earlier, Gehrig never appeared again. Two years later, he was dead of a disease known as amyotrophic lateral sclerosis, which had already begun to cripple him when he gave up his job in Detroit.

There was a rare twist to Gehrig's retirement from the line-up. Sitting in the lobby of the Book Cadillac Hotel that day was a gray-haired businessman from Grand Rapids, Michigan. He had come to Detroit to see the Yankees play. His name—Wally Pipp.

24
The Double
No-Hit

On the night of June 15, 1938, a crowd of 38,748 people came to Ebbets Field in Brooklyn to see the first baseball game played under lights in New York City. The major attraction was the novelty of night baseball. But a secondary attraction was a 22-year-old, left-handed pitcher for the visiting Cincinnati Reds, Johnny Vander Meer. Five days before the Brooklyn game, Vander Meer had pitched a no-hit game in Cincinnati and had beaten the Boston club, then known as the Bees, 3–0.

Vander Meer was in his first year in the majors and his no-hitter had made him the talk of the town. But while he had blinding speed, he was almost as wild as he was fast. And since he was new in the League, his knowledge of National League batters was limited. Some said his no-hitter was a fluke.

Johnny came from a family of Dutch descent in Midland Park, New Jersey, not far from Brooklyn, and a group of five hundred fans, including his parents, had come to see him pitch that night.

Max Butcher, a veteran right-hander, pitched for the Dodgers. In the third inning, Butcher got into trouble. With two men on, Cincinnati first baseman Frank McCormick hit a home run into the left-field stands. The next batter walked and came home on a double. So when Vander Meer came out for the fourth inning, he had a comfortable four-run lead.

Vander Meer warms up for a repeat performance.

In the first six innings no Dodger got as far as second base. Although Vander Meer had walked five batters, he had not given up a single hit. Under the artificial light his fast ball appeared even faster than usual and the Dodgers seemed helpless. No one had imagined that this inexperienced pitcher could repeat his no-hit performance. But by the end of the sixth even faithful Dodger rooters were pulling for Vander Meer. Few baseball fans ever see a no-hit game, but to see a pitcher hurl his second one in a row would be more than extraordinary.

In the seventh inning Vander Meer walked the first two batters. Now the crowd, sensing a Dodger rally, swung back to their home team in sentiment. But Johnny worked his way out of the situation.

He returned to superb form in the eighth inning. He struck out pinch hitter Woody English, retired the next batter on a grounder and struck out the third one.

As Vander Meer walked out to the mound for the ninth inning, Ebbets Field was swept by a tremendous ovation for him. Tension by this time had reached the breaking point. Every pitch was followed by a flutter of excited agitation in the stands.

Vander Meer handled the first out personally. The batter topped a bounder down the first-base side. Johnny fielded it and tagged him out on the first-base line.

Now, with a major league record a few pitches away, the young Cincinnati pitcher appeared to feel the pressure. He walked Babe Phelps, the Dodgers' portly catcher, who then left the game for a pinch runner. Despite his efforts, Vander Meer wasn't able to get his fast ball or his sweeping curve over the plate. The next two batters, Lavagetto and Camilli, walked. Now the bases were loaded with only one out. But the entire crowd, Dodger fans and all, stayed with the left-handed Red this time. Everybody except the Dodgers themselves wanted to see history created.

Center fielder Ernie Koy, an American Indian and a former football star, was the next batter. The right-handed Koy hit a slow roller to third baseman Riggs. It looked like a perfect setup for a double play, but Riggs, playing carefully for the force play at home plate, threw to the catcher so cautiously that there was no time to retire Koy, who was a swift runner, at first base.

Leo Durocher, the Dodger shortstop, was the next batter. He was a weak hitter, but he had a well-known ability to come through under pressure. He hit the first pitch like a rifle shot down the right-field line and the crowd leaped to its feet with a groan. But the drive curved foul into the stands.

The crowd was quiet as Durocher stepped back in to face Vander Meer. This time Johnny gave him

Teammates rush Johnny off the field after his second no-hitter in a row.

a fast ball. Durocher hit an arching fly ball to short
center field. Harry Craft, the center fielder, came
running and was there to catch it. With the bases
loaded, Vander Meer had put the Dodgers away. The
score: 6–0.

Great pitchers have come and gone since that night
in Brooklyn, but no one has ever pitched two no-hit
games in a row. Among those who remember Vander
Meer's feat, he is still known as Johnny "Double
No-Hit."

25
The Batboy Who Played

The year was 1952. Everywhere the Fitzgerald team of the Georgia State League traveled, Joe Reliford went along. Joe was batboy, clubhouse attendant, equipment boy and general handyboy. He was good-sized for a boy of twelve, almost big enough to be a member of the team. Sometimes the players let him sneak into the batting cage and get a few swings before a game. Joe could swing a bat well.

The players liked Joe because he was good-natured. And Joe liked the players because they were good to him and made him feel like one of them. For a lad in a small southern town, being batboy is a symbol of local stature. Everybody in Fitzgerald, and several other towns in the league, knew Joe Reliford.

Joe's favorite player was the Fitzgerald second baseman, Charlie Ridgeway. Charlie would often sit beside Joe on the bus as they rode through the night on their way home from a game in another town, and he would talk serious baseball with him. This made Joe feel grown up.

Joe liked speed in a baseball player and Ridgeway was the fastest runner in the Georgia State League. One season Ridgeway stole over sixty bases and Joe was certain that he would someday see his hero play in the big leagues. Charlie never made the majors, but before the end of the season, he got a promotion.

One day the president and manager of the Fitzgerald team, Ace Adams, called Ridgeway into the clubhouse and said, "Charlie, I've got a surprise for you. You're the new manager."

Adams had been managing the team and also trying to handle its business matters. The burden was too much for him, so he appointed Ridgeway his manager on the field.

Ridgeway had been the manager for a week when the Fitzgerald team was scheduled to play the Statesboro team, its rival in the pennant race. The Statesboro Elks Club was sponsoring a special "night" for the home team and a big crowd turned out for the game.

The sight of a filled park seemed to give the Statesboro players a big boost. They bombarded Fitzgerald with base hits, and Joe Reliford looked on sorrowfully as Charlie Ridgeway's new managerial career took a bitter turn. The score became so one-sided that the festive crowd, looking for other means of amusement, began jeering Joe as he trotted out to pick up the bats of Fitzgerald players.

By the eighth inning, Statesboro was leading by the score of 13–0. The fans began shouting the derisive ball-park cry, "Put in the batboy! Put in the batboy!"

By this time, Ridgeway was willing to do anything for relief. "Why not put in the batboy? If the crowd

wants a show, we'll give 'em a show," Ridgeway said
to himself.

Ridgeway called time and held a quick conference
with the umpire, a young man named Eddie Kubick.
"They're hollering for the batboy, Eddie," Ridgeway
said. "Our batboy's got on a uniform, and he swings
a pretty good bat. I've seen him in practice. What's
wrong with putting him in the game?"

"Nothing, as far as I know," Kubick said. "But if
you win the game, you'll have to forfeit for using an
ineligible player."

"The way things are going," Ridgeway said tartly,
"that isn't likely to happen. Reliford batting for
Nichting."

Ridgeway went back to the dugout and told Joe
to get a bat. He told Nichting, the leading hitter on
the team, to be seated.

"You're not serious, are you, Mr. Charlie?" Joe
asked.

"They've been hollering for a batboy," Ridgeway
said, "we'll give 'em the batboy. Get a stick and get
up there."

Joe hesitated a moment. Then he grabbed a bat
and walked up to the plate. The crowd howled.
Curtis White, the Statesboro pitcher, shook his head
in disbelief and looked at Kubick. The umpire motioned for the pitch as the announcement was made

over the public address system:

"Reliford batting for Nichting."

The crowd howled louder. Joe scratched the dirt with his shoe and waved the bat menacingly. White had a two-hitter going at the time and he was taking no chances. He cut loose with a good fast ball. Joe swung and connected. He smashed the ball toward the third baseman. It looked like a base hit, but the third baseman speared the ball and threw Joe out at first base by a step. Nevertheless, Joe's effort had been valiant, and the crowd now cheered him.

Ridgeway went all the way with his batboy. He threw him Nichting's glove and sent him to right field. One of the Statesboro players, Charlie Quimby, had a hitting streak of twenty-one games going into "Elks Night." While all his teammates had been feasting on Fitzgerald pitching, he was hitless as he came to bat for the last time in the eighth inning. He sent a sinking liner to right field that looked like a certain hit. Joe took out after the ball and just when it looked as though he would never make it, he stuck out his glove and made an acrobatic catch. Ironically Ray Nichting could never have made the catch. Not only was he a slow runner, but he led the league in errors by outfielders that season.

The Statesboro crowd stood and cheered the batboy as he ran in from the outfield with a broad grin on his face. Joe never got a chance to go to bat again, because the Fitzgerald team went down in order in the ninth.

It would have been a somber ride back to Fitzgerald that night but for the subject of Joe Reliford. The players, seemingly trying to forget their crushing defeat, carried on loudly and proudly about his part in the game.

"Better sign him to a contract, Skipper," one said to Ridgeway, "before he gets away."

"If he gets any better," said another, "he'll want a bonus."

Ridgeway raised his voice above the noise on the bus and said, "Fellows, if you never make it to the big leagues, you can always say you've done something no big leaguer has ever done. You've played with the youngest professional that ever played baseball."

He put his arm around Joe Reliford and gave him a big wink.

26

The Miracle of Coogan's Bluff

When men around New York City speak of the "Miracle of Coogan's Bluff," they can only be speaking of the year 1951 and the real fairy tale of the New York Giants. There will never be another "Miracle of Coogan's Bluff," because the Giants have moved to San Francisco and their old home park, the Polo Grounds, which was situated at the foot of Coogan's Bluff, has been torn down and replaced by apartment buildings.

The "miracle" belonged to Bobby Thomson, a 27-year-old third baseman and outfielder for the Giants. Thomson was born in Scotland, but his parents came to the United States when he was an infant. He had grown up on Staten Island, just across the bay from the heart of New York City.

He accomplished his feat at the Polo Grounds on October 3, 1951, but the story began almost two months earlier.

On August 11, the Brooklyn Dodgers, the Giants' most bitter rivals, led the National League by a margin of 13½ games. The Giants were in second place. The two teams had only thirty-eight more games to play and catching the Dodgers seemed utterly hopeless—to everyone except the Giants and their manager, Leo Durocher.

The next day, August 12, the Giants went to work on their "miracle." They won sixteen games in a row, cutting the Dodgers' lead to five games. It still seemed unlikely that the Dodgers could be caught. With their fine pitching staff and such sluggers as Gil Hodges and Duke Snider, the Dodgers gave the appearance of great strength. But the Giants had momentum and everything they touched turned to victory.

Finally on Friday, September 28, the Giants caught up with the Dodgers without lifting a bat. While the "miracle men" were idle, Brooklyn lost to Philadelphia, tying themselves with the Giants with two games left. Two days later, the season ended in a tie making a play-off necessary to determine the championship.

The play-off between the Giants and the Dodgers was as exciting as any World Series, and Ebbets Field, home of the Dodgers, was packed for the first game. Jim Hearn of the Giants pitched against Ralph Branca of the Dodgers and Hearn won with a five-hit game, 3–1. Thomson delivered the decisive blow, a two-run homer in the fourth inning. But this was only a warm-up for his "miracle."

In the second game, played at the Polo Grounds, Charlie Dressen, Brooklyn manager, surprised everyone by calling on a rookie pitcher, Clem Labine, just recently brought up from St. Paul, as his starter. Labine turned out to be the perfect choice. He shut out the Giants, 10–0.

In the deciding game, the Dodgers opened with a run in the first inning, taking advantage of veteran Sal Maglie's pitching wildness. In the second inning, something happened that seemed to tell the tense crowd that the Giants were through.

Bobby Thomson came to bat with Whitey Lockman on first base. Since Bobby had touched Branca for the big home run in the first game of the play-off, and since he had been the Giants' biggest hitter during their late-season comeback, excitement ran through the stands.

Thomson delivered. The Giants' third baseman lined a hit into left field. Rounding first base, he sensed that he had a chance to make it to second, and head down, he roared onward. Pulling into second, however, he came face to face with one of the most awful situations of his life. Whom should he meet, already standing safely on the bag, but Whitey Lockman. Lockman had played it safe. With the play on his side of the field he had chosen not to risk taking an extra base. All the Dodgers had to do was tag Thomson, and visions of a big Giant inning vanished.

In the seventh inning the Giants finally got to Newcombe for the tying run. It seemed that fortune was trying to make up to Thomson for the blunder he had pulled in the second inning, for it was he who hit a long fly ball scoring Monte Irvin from third.

Apparent disaster befell the Giants in the eighth inning, however. The Dodgers scored three runs and took a 4–1 lead. Spectators who liked to avoid the end-of-the-game rush began making their way toward the subway. The Giants didn't score in the last of the eighth, nor did the Dodgers in the top of the ninth.

In the last of the ninth, the Giants' Alvin Dark opened with a single off Newcombe. Don Mueller followed with a single that sent Dark to third. Irvin popped up for the first out but Lockman brought new hope to Giant fans by smacking a double that scored Dark and moved Mueller to third. The score was now 4–2, but the Dodgers needed only two more outs for victory.

Dodger Manager Dressen called time and went out to the mound to talk to Newcombe. The big Dodger pitcher stalked about, obviously unsettled and distressed. Failing to calm him down, Dressen motioned to the bullpen in distant left field, and out came Ralph Branca, his black windbreaker thrown over his shoulder. Bobby Thomson was the next batter. Although he had blasted a big home run off Branca two days previously, Dressen felt Branca was the man for the situation.

Thomson stepped into the batter's box, and Branca

delivered. It was a perfectly placed pitch, a fast ball that slipped over the outside corner of the plate for a strike.

Branca checked third base, now occupied by Clint

After a disastrous eighth inning had given the Dodgers a 3-run lead, Bobby Thomson belted his last-minute homer to win the pennant play-off, 5–4.

Bobby danced a jig on his way to home plate and a jubilant welcome.

Hartung, who was running for Mueller, and second
base, occupied by Lockman. Then he pitched. The
ball came in high, on the inside, out of the strike zone.
From his crouched position, however, Thomson took
a swing. At first the ball's flight indicated only a long
fly to left field, and the left fielder, Andy Pafko, drifted
back to take it. But the ball kept traveling and soon
Pafko was up against the wall.

As Thomson trotted into first base he turned and took a second look at the ball, then began jumping up and down. The ball had reached the stands—it was a home run!

Hartung scored and Lockman scored, and Thomson followed, dancing a jig down the third base line toward home. By the time he reached the plate, everybody in a Giant uniform, as well as a few over-zealous fans, had come to greet him, and a wildly jubilant celebration took place. With one blow, when all had seemed lost, Bobby Thomson had won the pennant for the Giants in their home at the foot of Coogan's Bluff. His run had made the score 5–4 and the play-off was over. Ralph Branca, who had stood on the pitcher's mound watching the flight of the drive, his body growing limp and his spirit faint, now turned and began the long, lonely walk to the club-house. As he turned, the number on the back of his uniform stood out as if lighted by neon: 13.

INDEX

(Page numbers in italics refer to photographs.)

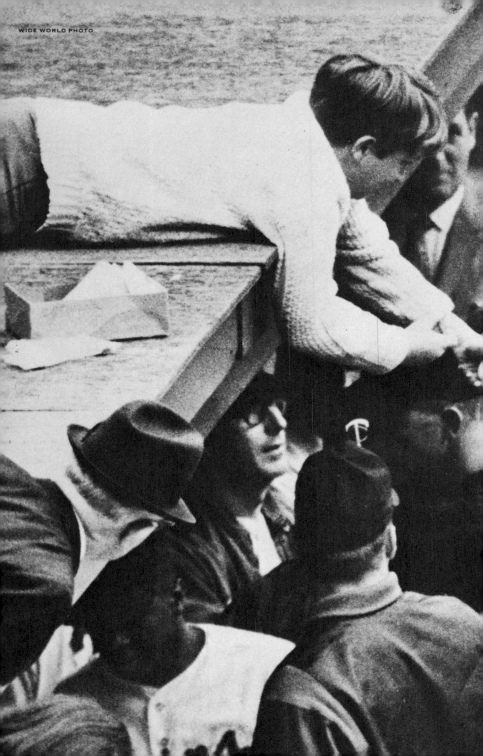

Fly Free

Fly Free

C.S. ADLER

COWARD-McCANN, INC.
NEW YORK

Acknowledgments

Thanks for information provided by Sue Clark,
benefactor of raptors,
and Geraldine Foster, teacher and wildlife lover.

Library of Congress Cataloging in Publication Data
Adler, C. S. Fly free.
Summary: Shy thirteen-year-old Shari, abused at home by a
mother who resents her, is befriended by a neighbor who
shares her love of birds and the out-of-doors.
[1. Child abuse—Fiction. 2. Birds—Fiction] I. Title.
PZ7.A26145F 1984 [Fic] 83-16599
ISBN 0-698-20606-1

For the best of mothers, mine.

Fly Free

One

Charlotte's voice startled Shari out of her daydream and nearly caused her to fall out of the tree.

"What are you doing up there? And why aren't you watching your little brother? I got to leave, and you better find him fast if you know what's good for you," Charlotte said.

Shari looked down into her mother's anger-flushed face and was tempted to retreat to higher branches, but deliberately disobeying Charlotte was too risky. Instead, Shari swung down from her seat in the notch between the trunk and the thick lower limb that jutted halfway across the backyard. She landed lightly beyond Charlotte's striking range.

"Big girl like you hanging out in trees like an ape. You ought to be ashamed of yourself," Charlotte said.

"Shari Ape Face, that's what I'm calling you from now on. Well, where's Peter?"

"I'll get him," Shari said and started off, anxious to get away before Charlotte asked again where he was, and Shari had to admit that she'd let him go to Mabel's store by himself.

Peter was six and would waste his spending money on what Charlotte considered junk—candy and gummachine toys. But this morning, he had told Shari earnestly, "I got to go alone. I'm a big boy now, and I got a right to go alone." Shari sympathized with his need for independence. Being five years younger than any other child in the family made it hard for him to grow up. Also, she knew that he didn't want her along today because he intended to buy her a belated birthday present. He'd been saving up for it. Usually he confided his plans to her before they could even qualify as secrets, but this time he hadn't. "You'll see," he had said. "I'm getting you something good."

Something to do with birds, she expected. He knew how much she loved birds. Last year, for her twelfth birthday, he'd given her a fluffy polyester chicken with a plastic beak and legs, not her ideal bird image, but she treasured it because it came from him. He was her special brother, her pair partner. Everyone in their family paired off. It was their mother, Charlotte, with their father, Zeke, then Doug and Walter, the two brothers who'd been born right after Shari and who were now twelve and eleven. She'd been odd man out until Peter came along six years ago.

Shari ran the quarter of a mile along the shoulder of the highway to Mabel's store. She called to Peter as soon as she got close enough to see him. He was talking to a boy more her age than his who was slouched against the scarred clapboard siding of Mabel's store. The boy had a sneer on his face that made Shari wish Peter were not such a wag-tail puppy of a boy that he would try to make friends with just about anybody.

"Peter," she called again, but still he didn't hear her. No surprise in that. Shari was always being told by teachers to speak up, but she couldn't do it. Quietness was part of her protective camouflage.

"My sister can," Peter was saying. "She could jump from this old roof to the shed easy."

"I'll bet," the mean-eyed stranger mocked. "Even a boy would need wings to jump that far."

"My sister can jump better than any boy. She can climb trees too, and she can even walk across a rope if it's tight enough."

"This your sister?" the kid asked.

Peter turned and saw her. A grin rounded his pudgy cheeks. "Shari, this kid don't believe me. You tell him. You can jump that far, can't you?"

"I don't know." She had no interest in proving anything to the unpleasant-looking stranger. All she wanted was to get Peter home before Charlotte got too angry. "Ma's been looking for you, Petey."

"I bet you couldn't even climb to the top of a roof that steep, let alone jump across to that shed," the kid taunted.

"Show him, Shari," Peter begged. "Show him how easy you can do it. Please!"

"She sent me to get you. She wants you home *now*," Shari said. No need to spell it out for him. Little as he was, he understood who would suffer if he didn't leave immediately.

She saw an uncertain flicker in his eyes, but he protested. "It'll only take you a minute. Come on. Show him, Shari."

Five minutes, she estimated and was tempted. She loved to climb and jump. It was as close to flying as she could get. The steep shingled roof of Mabel's general store would be easy enough to clamber up in sneakers, but jumping to the low shed off to one side could be tricky. She'd need a running start to clear the four or five feet of space between. While Shari considered, Peter said to her, "Guess who this kid's visiting, Shari?"

"I'm visiting my great aunt," the boy got in quickly, as if to ward off insult. "She lives back there." He jerked his head toward the run-down house across the highway and down in a hollow where the duck lady lived. There, hordes of noisy white ducks quacked around a pond behind the feather-strewn fence that protected them from the wheels of the trucks that sped past night and day.

"I'll do the jump after lunch," Shari decided.

"I'll be gone by then," the boy said. "My dad and me got to get to Burlington. But that's okay. I figured you couldn't do it. It'd take a circus guy, a trapeze artist, to jump that far."

"Shari could be in a circus if she wanted," Peter said.

"I can do it," she said impulsively. This was the closest to being a flyer she was ever likely to get.

Peter radiated pride, as if she'd already proven his boast, when she began to shinny up the drainpipe. No sooner did she reach the roof than she forgot him. She had this moment all to herself, the thrill of feeling her pliable, narrow body behave as if she were made of elastic instead of bones and muscle. She ran lightly up to the ridgepole and balanced there for a few seconds, breathing deeply of the pine- and juniper-scented Vermont woods spread out in great curves on the hillsides around her. She could taste summer in the wind as she looked back up the road to her own diminutive house tucked into the hillside. The giant green head of her favorite tree reared up behind her house, and near it lay the rusty sedan that Zeke still hadn't had time between long-distance truck hauls to fix for Charlotte. To the left below the duck pond, where a narrow road traced a thin line, the steeple of the Methodist church poked through surrounding greenery. If she were a bird, she would swoop from this roof down over the steeple and cruise over the lake where Zeke sometimes took them swimming when he was home long enough in the summers. If she were a bird, if only—

"You gonna jump or just take in the view?" the boy asked, squinting up at her.

The distance to the shed looked greater than it had seemed from below. Rusty nails stained the ragged asphalt shingles. Dark patches made her wonder how sturdy the shed roof was. If she broke through, Charlotte would make her pay for it. "Are you a girl or a monkey?" Charlotte might ask. And how could Shari pay Mabel for damaging her roof when she hadn't even been able to save enough money to replace the parakeet that her father had given her which had flown out her open bedroom window last summer?

Shari hesitated, but before she could change her mind, Peter urged, "Jump, Shari." And from down the road came Charlotte's shrill voice calling her name. Shari started. She hunched into herself, then backed up and sprinted along the ridgepole. She dove across the space between the two buildings. Her arms reached toward the shed, and she felt the joy of being suspended in air. For those seconds, she was a hawk soaring on wind currents high above the shirred green mountainsides, light and free and wholly beautiful. Then the palms of her hands took the abrasive blow of the landing. She did a forward roll so that she wound up with her weight evenly distributed, stretched out lightly on her back on the shed roof.

"See? Did you see that?" Peter was chortling down below. "My sister can climb and jump better than anybody."

Instantly she eased herself over to the edge and jumped to the ground. "We've got to get going, Peter. Don't you hear her?" She grabbed Peter's hand and began running, blind to the open-mouthed admiration of the stranger. All that mattered now was reaching Charlotte before she exploded.

Peter chugged along behind Shari, clinging to the cardboard tube he'd bought at Mabel's store and panting. He wasn't much of a runner. As Zeke said, it was Peter's mouth that ran best.

"We showed him, didn't we show him?" Peter said between gasps for breath when they reached the kitchen door of their house.

"Why do you care what that boy thought? He wasn't anything to you."

"No, he was just a big fuzz ball, nothing but a big old fuzz ball, but we showed him anyways," Peter insisted. Her thirteen-year-old wisdom bounced right off his rubber-skinned consciousness of the world. It frustrated her when she couldn't make him see things the way she did, but she had no time to try again before

Charlotte whipped the screen door open and confronted them.

"Well, you sure took your time getting here. I went down to the road and couldn't find you. Where were you?" Anger swelled the edges of her still-girlish prettiness so that she didn't look like the beauty queen Zeke claimed she could be.

"I got about the best-looking wife in Vermont," Zeke always said of Charlotte, "and sweet as Vermont's maple syrup too." Shari wondered how he'd see her if he stayed home with her more; but the trucking company he worked for kept him on the road most of the time, especially during the summer months when so much produce was harvested and shipped.

"Didn't I tell you I got to get my hair done this afternoon?" Charlotte said. "Think just because BeeJay is my friend it don't matter when I show up? You know it's not polite to be late for an appointment. You know she's got a business to run, and they're doing me a favor already having Marvin pick me up on his way back to the shop from lunch. A lot you care about anything I got to do. What were you doing? Swinging in the trees again, Miss Shari Lally, ape girl? And how did you cut yourself?"

Shari looked down at her hands. The right one was bleeding—from a nail on the shed roof probably. "I'll get a Band-Aid," Shari said.

"Put iodine on it. And Peter, you eat something quick. I'm taking you with me. You're going to the dental clinic today."

"Do I have to?" Peter asked. He was carefully pouring himself a glass of milk from the container in the refrigerator. Shari could see him as she reached for a

Band-Aid in the cabinet in the bathroom, which was next to the back door.

A car honked, a double beep of command from the road outside their house. The car couldn't take refuge in the driveway because Peter's hand-me-down fleet of dump trucks and wagons and cranes littered the blacktop there. Charlotte cursed and ran to the living-room window to wave at Marvin, then dashed back to tell Peter, "Forget that milk. You got no time to eat now."

"But I'm hungry!" Peter protested. His good nature depended on regular and frequent feedings. When hungry, Peter whined.

"Grab a banana and let's go," Charlotte said. "Shari, I told you to get his toys out of the driveway, didn't I? Now why can't you ever do like I ask you? People could get killed stopping on the road because they can't use our drive the way it's junked up with stuff. You get it cleared out by the time I get back or else. And don't forget the wash." She dashed out the front door, hauling Peter behind her and leaving the screen door wide open.

The peace of the empty house settled around Shari like balm. She felt sorry for her brother. Right now he'd be whimpering from hunger in the car between Charlotte and the gossipy Marvin, who co-owned the Shear and Shave Hair Cutting Parlor with his sister BeeJay. Shari hoped BeeJay or someone took pity on Peter and bought him a snack.

She drank the glass of milk he'd left and considered whether to make a baloney sandwich or her usual peanut butter. She didn't feel much like either. "Skinny as a wet cat," Charlotte called her, when she wasn't comparing Shari to an ape. "At your age I'd been wearing a bra for years." The comment had lacked the barb Charlotte had intended because Shari liked her narrow, supple body. She still daydreamed of being an Indian girl, invisible in the woods, at one with the lean trunks of the reeds, as long and straight as her dark brown hair. She practiced disappearing in classrooms too. There she sat silent and motionless, answering questions in a whisper so that teachers forgot her existence. Hers was usually the last name they learned, and Shari preferred it that way.

She wandered out the front door to consider the driveway her mother had told her to clear. Peter had dug a hole in the soft dirt where the blacktop had cracked apart. He had certainly made a mess.

She wished she could let everything stay where it was and steal an hour alone on the mountain for herself. It would be fun to explore that spot where the water burbled up through bare rock, icy cold even on the hottest summer day. Above that was a ledge too difficult for Peter to climb where she could sit and dangle her legs and contemplate the world below, so peaceful in its distance. No sense even thinking about it. To have escaped Charlotte's wrath this noon had been miracle enough for one day.

Abruptly Shari got to work. She piled the trucks in an empty carton under the carport. Doug and Walter hadn't shown up for lunch. She supposed they'd taken sandwiches along to their vegetable stand by the crossroads so that they wouldn't have to lose any sales by biking home before supper time. That would be Doug's idea. He was so intent on making money this summer that he didn't even take the time out for the ball games which used to be his whole life. As for Walter, he went along with whatever interested Doug, content so long as he could keep a book in his pocket and spend most of his time reading it.

The driveway looked fine when Shari finished. She was hot from working in the sun, so she climbed into her shaggy-leafed tree, up to the notch that fit her body like a contoured chair. Walter and Doug used this spot as a hiding place sometimes. They would shoot their peashooters or water guns from here. But mostly the tree was her place. Here she could relax into the airy sensations of sun and shadow, entertained by the warblers and the twits and tweets of chickadees. The trickling sweetness of time flowing by began to refresh her spirit as always.

She remembered the wash when it was too late. The slam of the car door and Charlotte's double-pronged laugh jolted Shari. Midafternoon, judging by the sun's position. They were back before she'd expected them.

"Shari, where are you?" Charlotte called. Her hair was set in frosted waves fixed with hair spray that she would not brush out for days. Shari liked Charlotte's hair best when rain made it curl in a fluffy cloud around her face. Shari liked her own reedlike body and didn't mind the penciled-on look of her features, but she wished she'd inherited her mother's hair. It was the only part of Charlotte she wished was hers.

In the kitchen, Shari saw the cardboard tube Peter had carried back from Mabel's store lying near the wall where everybody's muddy shoes and winter boots were dropped. She picked the tube up.

"That's your present. You didn't look at it yet, did you?" Peter asked as he trailed in after Charlotte, who went to look at her hair in the mirror in the bathroom.

"This is for me?" Shari asked, trying to sound surprised.

"I told you I was gonna get you a good present, but I didn't have enough money before. It's that poster with a bird on it."

"You mean the one with the hawk over the valley?"

"That's the one. You said you liked it."

"It's my most favorite. Oh, Peter, I can't believe you really got it for me."

"Well, I did." He beamed as he urged her to open it.

Charlotte came out of the bathroom and listened to Shari exclaiming over what a wonderful present the poster was, and how she didn't mind at all that it was three weeks late. The more fuss she made, the happier Peter looked.

"What'd you do about the wash?" Charlotte asked.

"I did the driveway," Shari said.

"Big deal. That took you about two minutes—"

"A lady at BeeJay's gave me a sugar bun," Peter interrupted, "and I didn't have to go to the dentist either, because the sign on the door said it was closed. And we drove past Walter and Doug. Boy, are they making lots of money! There was six cars at their stand."

"I'm going in to watch my soap," Charlotte said as if she were bored with the whole exchange. "And maybe I'll take a nap before dinner. You keep Peter out of the house, will you? You can do the wash later."

Shari couldn't believe her luck. Charlotte had given her a gift of sun-gilded hours in the woods. "Peter," Shari whispered, "let's hang up the poster tonight and go down to the stream and pan for gold now, okay?"

"Yeah," Peter said, his eyes widening with delight.

Panning for gold excited him more than just puddling around in the stream with her. It was one of the tricks she used to make the things she liked appealing to him.

Shari grabbed the sifter from under the scraggly forsythia bush, now summer green instead of spring golden.

"You going to borrow Mama's sifter again? She'll kill you, Shari," Peter said.

"I'll put up my invisible shield."

"But it didn't work last time."

"Sometimes I don't get it out in time."

"I don't like it when she hits you," Peter complained.

"Don't worry. She can't hurt me." Saying it helped her to believe it. Besides, going around scared all the time just spoiled the sweetness of the good moments, the free time when she could fly. As for the sifter, Shari needed it to keep Peter busy. He liked using equipment, whether in the soft dirt at the edge of the driveway or in the sandy bottom of the stream.

They walked one behind the other on the ill-defined path to the ravine where a stream rushed madly over fallen debris in spring, but was tame now in summer. This late in the afternoon, the bottom of the ravine was already shadowed in for evening.

"Maybe we should pan for gold tomorrow," Peter said cautiously.

"Come on; it's not that dark," she pleaded. "We'll only stay an hour."

He shrugged, already too old to own up to being scared. A year ago he would have, but he was tired of Doug's taunting him for being the baby and anxious to catch up with his older brothers. "You go ahead and

I'll follow," he told Shari. "I can get down okay by myself."

It was true. Going down, he relied on his bottom for security. It was on the climb up that he always hung on to some part of Shari as she guided them from rock to tree root to bush and he looked up fearfully at how far they still had to climb. He never looked back. She had convinced him not to.

Peter slid the last ten feet on his blue-jeaned butt, getting well coated with the mud at the edge of the stream. Shari made a mental note to rinse his jeans off with the garden hose before entering the kitchen. Charlotte took it as a personal attack if they tracked mud into the house. Last week when Peter had brought a turtle home, along with muddy grass, rocks and moss for its basin, Charlotte's punishing hand had lashed out quicker than Shari could duck. On her mother's orders, Shari had released the turtle in their backyard. But Peter sniffled and wept all through supper, until Charlotte finally relented and sent Shari to retrieve the creature. Walter and Doug had helped her search, but the turtle had made its escape for good. Peter had cried himself to sleep.

"Don't say I didn't try to get it back for you," Charlotte had said to him in the morning. "Maybe I'll get you some goldfish instead." She didn't, though. Charlotte disliked animals.

Peter squatted beside the stream with the sieve at the ready. "We can keep the gold if we find it, can't we?"

"Sure," Shari said. "This is our own place, Peter. Nobody comes here but us. Whatever we find is ours."

"Fishermen come though."

"Only on the other side of the bridge, across the highway, never here."

"And there's really gold?"

"Doesn't it look just like the picture I showed you in the library book where they were prospecting for gold in California?"

"Yes, but then why's nobody found any yet?"

"Because nobody but us has looked. Now concentrate." He set to work sieving the streambed as Shari's eyes followed a brown bird in the underbrush. She wondered what it was after in there—insects, seeds, material to line its nest? She could hear it skittering about, but couldn't see it anymore. If she were that bird, maneuvering through the underbrush—but it would have problems too, she thought. No way to escape them.

The burbling water hurried around rocks and logs and made sharp little rills before settling over deeper pools. A crow flapped from one side of the ravine to the other. Did it mind their presence? She had found a nest of cardinals last spring and had watched them raise their young, even witnessing the last baby's first flight. But when she tried to write about it for a school composition, it hadn't come out sounding like nearly the thrill it had been. The kind of joys she had were hard to share.

She was a person who liked being alone. At school, when she had a choice between working by herself or with a partner, she chose to work alone. Then she would finish quickly and use the leftover time to daydream or to sit back as if she were at a play and watch the others flirting and teasing and tormenting one another. All their spitball wars, note passing and tricks were interesting to observe, but she resisted any attempt to get her to participate. Her classmates knew she was a swift runner, good at gymnastics, and that she was quiet. They knew her name and that was enough. Total anonymity would have suited her better.

Once Shari's third-grade teacher, determined to wean her from her shyness, had given her a speaking part in a school play. She'd whispered her way through rehearsals, but the teacher wouldn't relent. Dressed as a fairy godmother on the day of the performance, with both her parents in the audience, Shari had been unable to utter a word.

"You embarrassed us to death, acting like a dummy in front of the whole school," Charlotte had scolded in the car on the way home.

Then Zeke had attempted to comfort Shari. "Don't feel so bad, baby," he said. "You looked mighty cute in your costume, and everybody got the idea without your saying anything anyway." He squeezed her shoulder, but he couldn't lessen her humiliation.

Nobody else in the family liked the things she liked or enjoyed being alone. Even Zeke, who had to spend long hours on the road in the cab of his truck by himself, said he depended on his C.B. radio, not just to keep in touch with other drivers for safety's sake, but for company. And if BeeJay, Charlotte's closest friend, was busy, Charlotte would summon Lina, whom she called "that boring potato sack" behind her back, to keep her company. If no one came to visit and Zeke wasn't home, Charlotte went to bed when her children did and left the TV on so that she could hear human voices in the house all night. The woods that attracted Shari frightened Charlotte.

Slowly, Peter and Shari worked their way down-stream to the narrowest part of the ravine, where the wrecked car of the robbers still lay with doors sprung open and front end crushed in. The police had chased the teenage robbers until their car had careened off the road above and torn a wayward path down the bare slope into the ravine. The boys had been lucky to escape alive.

"Tell me again how we'll spend the gold, Shari," Peter asked. Talk, even talk he had heard before, suited him better than the subtle song of the birds and wind and water.

"I told you," she said. "First thing we do after we stake our claim is get out a big bucket of gold nuggets and take it to the bank and open a savings account. Then we'll lend Zeke enough money so he can quit truck driving and buy a little business for Charlotte and him to work in together."

"And I get a two wheeler."

"The best two wheeler we can find, and those cowboy boots you wanted for last Christmas besides."

"And a beebee gun."

"Not yet. You're too young."

"And all the video games and my own TV."

"Yes."

"And you get a bird, Shari, a green one like Chirpy was."

"Blue this time," she said. "I could call him Starlight, or Blue Boy maybe." Her voice snagged on a memory that still had the power to hurt her. She looked at the uncompromising rocks, willing them to turn golden, and swallowed and said, "I'm going to buy an airplane too, a little one I can learn to fly by myself." That was her latest dream, replacement for her old desire to be magically transformed into a bird.

"You are?" He sounded alarmed. She had never told him that before.

"What's wrong with an airplane?" she asked. "Wouldn't you like it if I became a jet pilot?"

"I don't want you to fly away from here."

"What makes you think I'd do that?"

"Because."

"I won't leave you, Petey Pie. You don't have to worry," she promised.

He hugged her then, muddy hands and all. Except for Zeke, Peter was the only one who ever hugged her. Charlotte would sometimes take Peter onto her lap and cuddle him, but Shari couldn't remember the last time she and her mother had hugged or kissed.

To get to the smashed car, they had to cross the stream above the rapids where water thundered down even in summer. A tree straddled the stream conveniently, but one slip from its narrow trunk and the next landing could be on the rocks below the first six-foot drop. As usual, Peter squeezed his eyes shut and swore he wouldn't cross. As usual, Shari ran lightly across and back to show him how easy it was. Next she took his cold hands and coaxed him forward inch by inch as she backed across the log, as steady as if she were walking on level ground. She didn't forget to tell him how brave he was when they reached the other side.

"It's getting dark," he answered fretfully. "And I'm hungry."

"Not yet. A little longer," she pleaded, reluctant to return to the kitchen where Charlotte would soon be standing by the stove with a cigarette dangling from her sulky mouth as she cooked their dinner.

A catbird warbled throatily, then twittered an imitation of another bird's song as it bounced on a springy twig above them. "Listen to that, Peter," she said to distract him. "Doesn't that little gray bird sing better than anybody?"

The running brook chimed sedately, now that they'd left the falls behind. Leaves hummed wind lullabies. Feeling happy, Shari followed the slanted sun rays to where the carcass of the robbers' car lay like a crushed animal, its nose to the stream edge. Something glinted in the tangle of weeds there. She bent and picked up a large chunk of glass. When she washed it in the stream, she caught her breath as the sleek, curved neck of a swan with swept-back wings emerged. "Petey, look what I found."

"Gold?" he asked.

"Almost." The smooth weight of the bird nestled on her palm as if it belonged there as she showed it to him.

"Is it a treasure?"

"*I* think so." She set it in his cupped hands. "Isn't it marvelous, Petey?"

"No," he answered honestly. "It's just a glass bird."

"But it's so beautiful," she said, "and it's not chipped or scratched or anything." She took the swan back into her own hands, and again it fit into her palm and warmed into life as she held it. "I think it's something precious."

"Can we sell it and get rich?" Peter asked.

"I'd rather keep it," she said. She held the bird against her cheek and closed her eyes. "I never owned anything this pretty," she murmured. Not the stone with the red grains that might be garnets, not the butterfly pin without a back that Peter had found and given her, nor the feather from the tail of the green parakeet who'd disappeared into the woods last summer. Nothing had ever come into her hands as lovely as this graceful bird.

Peter's stomach rumbled out loud. "I'm starving," he complained. "And it's getting really dark down here."

"We'll go," she said apologetically. He hadn't eaten much for lunch today. She took him by one hand, carefully holding the swan in the other, and began immediately to lead him home.

Two

After the gray and brown halftones of the ravine, the lemony gleam of the late afternoon made Shari and Peter blink. Only when they reached their own backyard, where the mountainside blocked the last slanted sun rays and turned tree trunks into black pillars, did they find evening again. Peter hurried toward the lighted window of their kitchen, eager for the comforts of food and family awaiting him inside, but Shari hung back. For her, the glowing square of window was like an open fire, both attraction and threat.

The car in their driveway belonged to Charlotte's friend Lina. When Lina's husband went on the road with his sample case, she often dropped in to "visit awhile" and stayed on through supper if Charlotte's need for company was great enough to allow that. Lina would sit placidly clucking in sympathy while Charlotte talked at a fast trot. What she told the childless, bulky Lina was the latest edition of old news—how Charlotte wished Zeke made more money so they could afford some item Charlotte desired, and how lonely she got with him gone all the time, and what rotten luck she had being stuck in the country with four kids to drive her up a wall. After Lina left, Charlotte would complain that entertaining that woman gave her a headache, but she couldn't be too choosy about her friends here in the middle of nowheresville.

Tonight, as Shari lingered outside the door, she heard her mother going on again about how she'd planned a career in fashion, had an eye for it and could have become a buyer if she hadn't married Zeke and gotten pregnant instead.

"No fashion career around here, that's for sure," Lina agreed.

"I'll say. And Zeke don't want me to work anyways. Remember when I took that job as hostess in the Blue Hill Hotel? And Zeke got so mad at me I had to quit? Of course, the place only lasted one summer anyway, but what got Zeke was he thought the owner had his eye on me."

"Maybe he did," Lina said. "You don't look like the mother of four kids."

"No, I've kept my figure. I can eat whatever I want and never put on weight."

"Well, you burn it up with nerves. Nervous energy burns up fat. Take me. Not a nerve in my body. Everything I put in my mouth just stays with me." She patted her lumpy thighs as if she were proud of them.

"I bet you eat more than you think you do, Lina."

They argued mildly about that for a minute, and then Charlotte said, "Where's that sister of yours, Pete? She stuck up in a tree somewhere?"

"She's coming," Peter said. "Ma, can I have a can of spaghetti? I'm hungry."

"Don't bother me now. Can't you see I'm talking with Lina? Go watch some TV until your brothers get home. . . . That Shari. People say it's good getting the girl first so she can help out with the younger kids, but Shari don't do a thing around this house unless I'm right on her tail to make her."

"Don't she take care of her little brother all the time?" Lina said. "You got to give her credit for that."

"Credit? What for? She don't mind having him follow her around like a puppy. And who else is going to pay attention to her? She don't have a friend her own age. Now I ask you, Lina, is that normal? A girl her age so shy she can't even open her mouth in school."

"But she does all right in school anyway, don't she?"

"Well, sure. She's smart enough. All my kids are smart."

"That's not so great for you, Charlotte," Lina said. "That just means you got to figure on paying their way through college."

"We're not sending these kids to college, not on what Zeke makes," Charlotte said. "Besides, Walter's the only one who likes school, and he can just win himself a scholarship if he wants to go. You can bet Doug's not going to waste four more years in some classroom when he can be out hustling. He'll probably be making a fortune by the time he's old enough for college. You know what he told me the other night? 'Mama,' he said, 'when I'm rich, I'm going right out and buy you a new car.' That's what he said."

"What about Shari?" Lina asked.

"Oh, Shari. She'll get married like I did, or else end up cleaning out motel rooms or waiting tables."

"She could be a teacher or something," Lina said.

"Shari? Don't make me laugh. She couldn't get her mouth to open to a stranger to save her life."

"Shari wants to be a pilot," Peter's voice piped up defensively. "She wants to fly jet planes."

"Fly? Where'd she get a notion like that?" Charlotte said sharply with a note of fear in her voice. She paused, then said, "Anyways, you got to go to school to be a pilot, and Shari's going to work as soon as she finishes high school."

"What about you, Charlotte?" Lina said. "You could find a job."

"I could, huh? Doing what?"

"Salesclerk in the mall maybe."

"Oh, sure. They're just waiting to hire a housewife with no experience, and besides, how am I going to drive forty minutes each way when there's ice and snow on the roads and my car don't run half the time? Think I haven't thought about that mall? But until I get a car that works right, forget it."

"Yeah, well, working is not all it's cracked up to be anyways. Who wants to get up and get dressed early every morning?" Lina said. "Me, I'm so glad I can just roll over and sleep as long as I like."

"That's because you're lazy, Lina. I'm not lazy. . . . Where *is* that girl? Mooning around in the woods somewheres?" Charlotte said angrily. Being with Lina always made her irritable after a while. "That girl's never around to help me. All she thinks about is herself."

"It's funny," Lina said, "how the boys are the spitting image of Zeke and Shari don't look like you nor him."

"She takes after Zeke's family," Charlotte said, and added, "Listen, if you're not staying for dinner, I better start getting something for the kids. The boys are going to be hungry working that stand all day."

Lina ignored the hint. Her pillowlike nature seemed immune to insult. "Don't mind me. I'll just sit here and watch you work. I never mind watching someone else work."

"It makes me nervous to be watched," Charlotte said. "It was nice that you dropped by, Lina. I'll walk you to your car."

The sound of a chair scraping on the vinyl floor was followed by the slower sounds of Lina rising reluctantly to leave.

Shari took a deep breath. When Zeke got home, she would have to ask him if it was true that you had to go to school to become a pilot. She didn't want to clean motel rooms or wait on tables for a living.

As Charlotte ushered Lina out the front door, Shari slipped into the kitchen. She began setting the table immediately so that her mother couldn't find any fault with her.

"So, you finally got home," Charlotte said when she returned. "Where were you all this time?"

"Just outside."

The back door burst open and Doug and Walter piled in. Doug dropped into a chair at the kitchen table. He lay on the chair like a plank, with his head on the back and his legs stuck straight out, just the way Zeke did. "Boy, am I beat. When are we going to eat?" Doug said.

Walter was gulping water from the kitchen faucet.

"I haven't started dinner yet, so don't bug me," Charlotte answered. "How about if I open a couple of cans of spaghetti?"

"Not again, Ma," Doug said.

"Well, don't blame me. You can't expect me to get to the supermarket without a car."

"We got some tomatoes and squash we didn't sell that's only a little bruised," Walter said. "Don't we have any hamburger meat?"

Charlotte shrugged and went to the refrigerator.

"You going to take us to the bank so we can make a deposit soon?" Doug asked.

"I'll try and get BeeJay or Marvin to give you a ride."

"What about Lina?" Doug asked.

"Lina! I couldn't stand another hour in that woman's company this week, and besides, I don't like owing her favors."

"Hi, guys," Peter called brightly from the living-room doorway. "Did you sell a lot of food?"

"Best day all week, better than last Saturday," Doug said. "My suppliers didn't have hardly nothing to take back. It all got sold."

"If you're so rich, big shot, how about treating us all to dinner out tonight?" Charlotte said, smiling.

"I told you, Ma," Doug said. "You got to have money to make money, and I can't have it if I spend it right off."

"Stingy," Charlotte teased, but her eyes were admiring as she looked at her solidly built son, who had

Zeke's brown eyes and broad cheekbones. Shari finished setting the table and positioned herself in the doorway beside Peter, who stood listening to the conversation.

"You'd have your own money if you'd stop smoking so much," Doug said to his mother. "And then if you invested what you saved with me, I'd give you a good return and you'd have more."

"I don't smoke," Charlotte said. "I only take a puff once in a while for my nerves."

"You promised Zeke you'd stop," Walter reminded her.

"And who says I haven't. What am I, surrounded by spies, like in Russia? My own children spying on me? And now I suppose you're just waiting to tell your daddy that I'm smoking up a storm!"

"We won't tell if you help us get a ride to the drag race Saturday night," Doug said.

At first, Charlotte objected that Doug and Walter were too young for Saturday-night drag races, but when Doug explained his scheme for selling Kool-Aid to the little kids there, Charlotte looked tempted, even though that was an illegal transaction by track rules. Her green eyes narrowed, and a smile twitched the corners of her lips. "How'd you get so smart, Doug? I bet you *do* wind up rich someday."

"Shari and me are going to get rich, too," Peter said, suddenly inserting himself into the conversation. "We're going to find gold in the ravine."

The hoots of laughter from his brothers and mother wiped the brightness from his face. "Anyways, we did find something there," he said.

"What'd you find, a diamond ring?" Doug jeered.

"It was nothing," Shari threw in desperately, seeing the danger at once.

"But you said—" Peter accused her.

"Let's see what you found, for heaven's sake." Charlotte flicked her lighter open and lit a cigarette, sucking in her cheeks. She left the refrigerator and sat down at the table.

"Show it to Mama. You've got it, Shari," Peter said. He was eager to measure up to his brothers in his mother's eyes.

Cornered, Shari untied the bandanna by which she'd secured the glass bird to a loop of her jeans. The bird looked iridescent in the lamplight, the curves of its neck and wings as slippery with light as a stream of running water. She set it onto her mother's palm, holding her breath in the hope that Charlotte wouldn't see it as valuable enough to claim. Charlotte set her cigarette down in the misshapen ceramic ashtray Lina had made for her and turned the bird around and around in the pink, scoop-nailed ends of her fingers. "It's pretty," she announced. "It could be crystal. I seen something like it in the mall in the fancy shop."

"Is it a treasure?" Peter asked hopefully.

"Where'd you kids find it?" Charlotte wanted to know.

"In the stream, down from where the bridge crosses," Shari said.

"Finders keepers," Peter thought to say.

"You took your little brother down that steep gorge? Don't you have more sense than to take him to such a dangerous place?" Charlotte demanded.

"It's not dangerous," Shari said.

"And what are you going to do when he falls and breaks his neck? Tell me how sorry you are then?"

"I won't let him fall."

"You just better not. . . . I can't believe you found this just laying there in the stream," Charlotte said.

"Right where the robbers' car is wrecked," Peter assured her.

"But it wasn't in the car. It was in the stream," Shari qualified.

"So that's it," Charlotte said. "It was part of what those boys stole from that woman that lives alone on the mountain—what's her name again? The one that don't come from around here."

Shari shrugged for answer. Her fingers gripped the back of a chair while her eyes held on to the swan pincered between Charlotte's shell-tipped fingers.

"Her name's Mrs. Wallace," Walter said. Walter remembered everything. He could recite the plots of dozens of science fiction books and recall all the characters' names.

"The newspaper said a lot of stuff they took from her had only sentimental value. She collected things from where she'd lived all over the world," Charlotte mused. "It might be worth something to her to get this back."

"Please," Shari said, "can I have my bird now?"

"It's not yours," Charlotte snapped. "Don't you know you can't keep what's not yours?"

"But I found it."

"Didn't you hear what I just explained to you, dummy? . . . Listen, you go up there tomorrow, and here's what you do. You don't let on you found it. Just describe it and ask if it's hers and if she'd pay a reward to get it back. Say you could get it for her if there was a reward." Charlotte studied Shari, who stood helplessly gripping the chair back. "Are you paying attention to me?"

"Please, Mother," Shari whispered. "Let me keep it."

"What would Zeke say if he heard you wanted to keep something that's not even yours? I'm ashamed of you."

"It's not stealing if you find something and keep it," Shari dared to argue.

"It is if you know who the owner is," Charlotte said. "Listen, if she gives you a reward, you can keep half. Ask her for five dollars. Tell her you'll get it back to her for five. Okay?"

Shari turned her back on her mother in despair. If Zeke were home—but he wasn't. There was no one to whom Shari could appeal.

"What's the matter with you?" Charlotte asked irritably. "You're such a weird kid. I'm offering you half. Isn't that fair enough?"

It struck Shari that Charlotte would never expect Doug and Walter to give her half of anything they found, so why expect it of Shari? But that hardly mattered. Shari was used to Charlotte's unfairness. It was having to give up the bird that hurt. "May I have it in my room just for tonight?" she asked, avoiding her mother's eyes.

"Why not?" Charlotte was agreeable now that she'd won. "Listen, if she won't pay any reward, you just keep the thing as far as I'm concerned."

"But you said it's hers."

"So what? Didn't you find it? You didn't *take* it, did you?"

Charlotte's sudden shift in judgment was too abrupt for Shari to follow—another case where Charlotte set the rules to suit herself. Full of energy and cheerful now, she began pulling food out of the refrigerator saying, "I think I got some chopmeat here somewhere if it hasn't gone bad yet. Get me the tomatoes and squash, Walter. Come on, Shari. Help me get this supper started."

After the dishes were done, Shari left her family sprawled in the living room watching television and took the bird up the uncarpeted stairs to her room. No gleam in it now. Charlotte's touch must have dulled it. The hand that had opened the bedroom window last summer had long pointed fingernails. Shari boxed the knowledge away fast along with all the other hidden items in the attic of her mind. It was dangerous to know, dangerous because knowing might loose the anger, and what could Shari do with it then? All the pinches and slaps, all the razor-blade words, all the unfairnesses had to be boxed and forgotten for safety's sake.

She could have told her seventh-grade English teacher that that was where her childhood had gone. It was locked away so that Shari couldn't remember any experiences to write in the journal she had been required to keep for class.

"Such an easy assignment, Shari. Just to write about something you remember from when you were little. *Everybody* has some memories," the teacher had said.

"But I don't," Shari had answered truthfully.

On the next report card, the teacher had written under "comments" in the behavior section, "Shari's shyness makes her appear less socially mature than other girls her age. She needs to learn to relate to others better and to express herself more openly both orally and in writing."

"What kind of garbage is this?" Charlotte had said when she saw the report card. Instead of being furious with Shari, Charlotte had called the teacher and asked, "What do you mean, not socially mature? Shari don't need to go around acting like a sixteen-year-old and wind up pregnant like some other girls her age I could name. There's nothing wrong with her. Why shouldn't she keep to herself instead of associating with the trash you got in that school?"

Shari couldn't remember another time that Charlotte had stood up for her, and she couldn't fathom why Charlotte had chosen to this time, but then her mother's moods had always been unpredictable.

Her small, bare room sloped to the shape of the roof on the side where her battered dresser stood. A bed fitted below the window on the second wall. Zeke had put a clothes pole and shelves along the third wall for her belongings. Shari tacked the poster Peter had given her at the narrow end of the room where she could lie in bed and look at it. It was her favorite birthday present, she had told Peter. Last year her favorite present had been the live green-and-yellow parakeet Zeke had brought home to her. She still had the cage. It stood empty on the shelf above her winter boots and next to the toy record player that didn't work, and the broken doll with the voluminous lace skirt that Zeke had brought her years ago from one of his long-distance hauls. She had never much liked dolls, but anything Zeke gave her held the warmth of his affection for her, and so she treasured all his presents.

She sat on her bed, leaning against the window frame. Moonlight fell on the crystal bird in her hands. Tomorrow she had to return it to the lady who owned it—Mrs. Wallace. "It doesn't matter," Shari whispered, trying to convince herself. "It doesn't matter that it isn't mine."

Long ago she had learned to shield herself against pain when her mother hit her, but the nonphysical hurts were hardest to deny. "It doesn't matter," she repeated, sealing off her heart. To feel nothing was better, to remove herself so that the body that was there didn't hold her anymore. Then after a while the danger would go away, and if she was reminded of the hurt, it would be just another item to box away.

The bird glistened in the moonlight. It nestled in the palm of her hand like a comforting charm that promised good fortune. The night air rustled with the sounds of wind-stroked leaves and the rasping hum of insects. A birdcall curled musically through the darkness.

She slept and dreamed that she was drifting through her bedroom window, holding the crystal bird, whose outstretched wings were beating in long slow strokes against the night air. She felt herself rising through the fingering leaves of her tree until the bird passed the topmost twigs and she could see the stars far and away above her. Then she climbed onto the bird's back. It had grown to an enormous size, and its wings shimmered with moonlight.

The cool wind swished past as the crystal bird sailed through the night, more magnificent than the hawks whose proud domination of the sky she had envied as they hovered over the valley. Jewel clusters beneath her were the lights of houses, and the twin diamonds and rubies strung sparsely in a straight line were the head- and taillights of the cars passing on the highway below.

Joy fluttered inside her. She was flying, flying, flying as she had always dreamed, where no earthly thing could touch her, free of all bounds. If she could have, she would have sailed through the blackness of space through aeons of time to reach the constellations of stars overhead, so powerful did she feel as she swooped through the night, skimming the mountain-tops, soaring gloriously above them. Around and up and down and around again in great swirls of motion, like the tilt-a-whirl Zeke had taken them on at the county fair.

She awoke the next morning with the exhilaration of her passage still fresh, feeling renewed.

Three

"Come on, kids," Charlotte yelled. "Get down here for breakfast. I got a surprise for you today."

Shari sat up in bed wondering what could have caused the happy caroling of her mother's voice. Could Zeke have called to say he was coming home sooner than they expected? Or was the surprise just an invitation from BeeJay? Last month BeeJay took the whole family to the petting zoo at the shopping mall, and she had even bought an entrance ticket for Peter. Charlotte had gone inside with him while the rest of them watched the animals through the chain-link fence. Nice, but not as good as having Zeke come home.

Shari picked up the crystal bird and looked at it. Today she had to return it to Mrs. Wallace, unless some-

thing lucky happened. If Zeke was coming home,
Charlotte might just forget the bird. Or Zeke might say
Shari didn't have to return it. Shari wondered if he'd
think she had to just because she knew who the real
owner was. Probably he would say she should. That
was the honest thing to do.

Shari put on yesterday's cutoff jeans and a tee shirt
Walter had outgrown. It had a cartoon of Roadrunner
on it and was getting nubbly, but had no holes yet. She
brushed her hair, undisturbed by the lack of a mirror
in her room. Charlotte had offered to get her one for
her birthday last year, but Shari had asked for money
to spend on her parakeet instead. "That's the last pet
we're having in this house!" Charlotte had said after
Chirpy flew away. She'd been angry at Shari for mooning by her open window all week in the hope that he'd
return.

"I got enough human animals to take care of around
here," Charlotte had complained to Zeke. "No more
birds, or dogs either."

Walter had protested that it wasn't his fault that his
mixed-breed shepherd had bitten Peter, and he
couldn't help it that the dog got killed chasing a car
down the highway or that Shari's bird flew away.

"No more pets," Charlotte had repeated, and Zeke
took her side as usual.

"After all," he told Walter, "I'm gone most of the
time, and your mother's stuck with all the headaches.
You got to understand, Walt; she's got more than she
can handle as is."

Zeke had a lot of sympathy for his wife. "Don't take
what your mother says too hard," he'd told Shari once

when he heard Charlotte picking on her. "She don't mean half what she says. It's her nerves, that's all."

Charlotte was bouncing about energetically as Shari entered the kitchen. "So what if you don't open your stand one day," she was saying to a sour-faced Doug as she fixed his eggs at the stove. "How often do we get an invitation to go swimming anyways? You're only twelve years old, kid. Live a little."

Doug's hammer-ended chin set stubbornly in his broad face, but he said nothing.

"*I* want to go, Ma," Walter said through a bite of hamburger roll oozing jam. "But my cutoffs are too full of holes to swim in."

"Well, find something else to wear," Charlotte said. "I'm not sewing up those crummy cutoffs again."

"Then I'm not going." Walter folded his arms across his chest and shoved himself back from the table as if to remove himself from the family.

"I can't believe you kids!" Charlotte said. "BeeJay invites us all to the lake with her and you sit there and give me a hard time about it. Listen, for all I care, you can all stay home and I'll go without you."

"What about me?" Peter demanded. "I haven't been swimming all summer."

"I'd like to go," Shari said quietly.

"Well, hurry up and get ready then," Charlotte said. "BeeJay'll be here in a few minutes, and we got to fix some lunch to take."

"I can't go without my cutoffs," Walter said. Lately he'd become self-conscious about his bulky body. He insisted on keeping his hair long enough to cover his open-hinge ears and would only wear particular items of clothing that he thought suited him.

"You could wear my shorts," Shari offered. "They'd fit you, and I'll wear my old shorts to swim in."

"I'm not wearing girl's pants." Walter looked horrified.

"They were Doug's originally," Shari pointed out to him.

"We'll buy drinks at the lake," Charlotte muttered to herself as she stuffed bread and baloney and mustard and peanut butter and jelly, along with a knife for spreading and cutting, into the white Styrofoam cooler.

"My suppliers will get mad if I'm not there when they deliver the stuff I'm supposed to sell for them," Doug said.

"No, they won't. Just leave a sign. You can tell them your mother made you go. You're only a kid. What can they expect?" Charlotte said.

Abandoning the toast she had made for herself, Shari ran upstairs to change her clothes and bring her cutoffs down to Walter. She liked the lake, enjoyed basking in the sun, listening to waves slap hollow sounds from the oil drums that buoyed up the raft on which she lay. When she got back to the kitchen, Walter took the cutoffs without a word and went into the bathroom. Doug was on the phone talking to the lady who grew the tomatoes he sold.

"Don't tell anyone I'm wearing your cutoffs," Walter said to Shari when he came out.

She remembered the time Zeke had caught Walter reading a book as he sat beside Doug, who had the TV going at top volume. "Walter, did you learn how to read while riding your bike yet?" Zeke had joked. "Figure out how to read in the dark?" Walter had been so embarrassed he'd stuffed his book behind the cushions in the sofa and hadn't read another thing for a day. He couldn't take teasing, but Shari wished she could escape into books the way he could. When his eyes hunted back and forth across a page, he was oblivious to everything else. He read at night too, in the unfinished attic room space he shared with Doug and Peter, when everyone in the house besides her was asleep.

"What do you find in all those books?" she'd asked him, but he had no words to tell her. Like her, he took in a lot but let out little.

BeeJay honked the horn of her little red car with the black racing stripes.

"Lock the back door," Charlotte yelled and ran outside with the picnic box.

Peter slipped his hand into Shari's. "I don't need my water wings this year. I'm going to really swim."

"Wait," Shari said, remembering. "I'll get the inner tube." She ran to the carport where she'd last seen the tube, found it under the tangled garden hose and dashed to BeeJay's car with it. The tube would be fun for all of them.

Peter was fidgeting outside the car. Everybody else was already in it. As soon as Shari saw BeeJay's clumsy black Labrador retriever on the backseat between Doug and Walter, she understood.

"All right, you can sit up front with me if you're such a little scaredy cat," Charlotte was saying to Peter.

"I'm not getting in no car with that dog," Peter whined.

His fear was so huge Shari could almost see it. Ever since he'd been bitten by Walter's shepherd, he'd been afraid of big dogs. He would need to be protected from the restless BoBo. The dog's head hung over the

front seat, red tongue flopping while he nudged first
BeeJay and then Charlotte for attention.

"All right then, Peter," Charlotte said ominously.
"You can just stay home." Tears spilled from Peter's
eyes, but he didn't budge. "Shari, you stay with him,"
Charlotte said. "We don't need to be crowded in this
car for a kid who don't even appreciate going."

"That's the ticket, Charlotte," BeeJay said. "No
spoiled brats on this trip." BeeJay revved the engine,
grinning her rubber-mouthed grin.

Charlotte lifted tumbling locks from the back of her
neck as if she were already getting hot and uncomfort-
able. "Listen, Shari, you can fix a can of tuna fish or
something for lunch, and don't forget to see that lady
like I told you."

Shari flinched. From treat to tribulation faster than
the eye could follow. It had happened before, but that
didn't relieve her disappointment now. The car left
dust clouds on the road behind it. Peter was still crying
bitterly when the dust had settled.

"Come on, Petey," Shari said, letting her anger go to
concentrate on his misery. "We'll have a good time in
the woods by ourselves."

"But I wanted to go to the lake."

"Me too, but we can't; so we won't fuss about it. Let's
try and have fun anyway."

Her resolve was only shaken when they tried to get
into the house and found it was locked front and back.
Charlotte had the key with her. Shari's own key was
upstairs on her dresser.

"How're we going to eat?" Peter asked. Alarm dried
up his tears. Not to eat for a day was worse for him
than missing out on a swim.

"Don't worry. Mabel will let us have some doughnuts or something, and we can pay her tomorrow. You can't be hungry anyway. You just had breakfast. Let's go dig for gold again. Then we can sneak up on Mrs. Wallace's house and spy on her to see if she's nice."

"Why do you care if she's nice?" Peter asked.

"I'm not going to let her have the bird back unless she's nice."

"Mama will get mad at you if you don't."

"We'll see," Shari said, glad that she'd managed to distract him from his disappointment. "Come on. It's a long way up the mountain to her house."

He looked down the road longingly, but BeeJay's car had gone. Finally he sighed and even dredged up a smile for her as he said, "Okay. Let's go."

"You really are growing up, Peter," Shari said in praise of his quick adjustment.

They descended into the ravine and crossed the rapids, but before stopping to pan for gold, Peter suggested they do their spying on Mrs. Wallace first. "If she's nice, maybe she'll give us something to eat."

Shari laughed. "What kind of spies get invited in for a snack, Pete? She's not supposed to know we're spying on her."

"We'll see," Peter said in an echo of her own voice.

To get to Mrs. Wallace's, they had to climb the far wall of the ravine to reach a side road up the mountain. A projecting ledge of rock made a lip along the top edge of this wall of the ravine. Peter balked when they got to it. "I'm not climbing over that," he said. "No way." He looked nervously over his shoulder at the gravelly descent to the stream, which seemed forever below them.

"It's not as bad as it looks," Shari said. "I'll go first and find the toeholds."

"No," Peter said. "I can't do it. I'll fall."

"Relax," she said. "Soon as I'm up, I'll lower something you can hold on to. I didn't ever let you fall, did I?"

She left him clinging to a wedge of rock and twisted shrub and pulled herself from bare toehold to bare toehold, up and over the ledge, grasping exposed tree roots where she could. At the top, she lay belly down with her head hanging over the edge to tell him, "See, it's not so hard. I'll get something to lower to you so you can hold on as you climb up."

"I can't, Shari," he whined. "I'm scared."

"Want me to come back down and you can hold on to me as you come up?"

"I'm no good at climbing."

"Sure you are. Your only problem is your muscles aren't strong enough yet, but when you're older, you'll be as good a climber as me."

"No, I won't. I'm never going to be good at nothing. I wish I never got born into our family."

"You don't want me for a sister anymore?"

He considered that, looking troubled as he made up his mind. Finally he took a deep breath and said, "You better help me up there so I don't fall." Then he looked down fearfully to where the stream rushed over rocks and branches below them.

"Be right back," Shari said and hurried to find a strong, thin tree limb that she could reach down to him. Fortunately, she didn't have to go far. This back road was so untraveled that broken tree branches from last winter's storms still lay on its shoulders. Peter took the end of the branch she thrust toward him in both hands and clung for all he was worth as she hauled him up, but he did help by using his feet for climbing when she asked him to. She would not have been strong enough to pull him up otherwise.

"There," she said jubilantly, when they were resting side by side on top of the rock. "I told you it wasn't so hard."

"I did it," he said proudly.

She smiled and hugged him and agreed, "Yes, you did. Didn't I tell you you're getting to be a big boy?"

He hugged her back cozily, the way he always had, and she was glad he didn't feel too grown up for hugging.

They walked up the shady side of the macadam mountain road until they came to the dirt road marked private. Mrs. Wallace's name was on a post beside it. Two tire-track ruts with a weed-grown hump between them led up steeply through overgrown woods and fields of blackberry and mullein and goldenrod.

"What if she sees us?" Peter asked.

"We'll tell her we're looking for something," Shari said, and tried to think of what. She wasn't good at white lies. She hated talking to adults. Shyness made her voice disappear, and she often blurted out things that didn't sound right before dashing off in embarrassment.

"We could just tell her we got lost," Peter suggested.

"We could," Shari said, squeezing his hand gratefully.

"I can talk to her," Peter offered. "I like to talk to people."

"You're good at it," Shari agreed, "better than me."

She took a deep breath of spicy juniper and scented field flowers and admired the clump of tousled birches. A chipmunk skittered past them to the safety of a rock pile. Its golden brown body wore a flag of black and white stripes. "Everything's so pretty in the woods," Shari said.

"Are we almost there?" Peter asked. The woods had never much interested him.

"Must be." Shari hoped so for his sake.

As they rounded the last curve in the road, the house appeared. It was a sturdy wooden cottage with a steeply pitched roof like a witch's hat. They recognized Mrs. Wallace's pickup truck in front of the open garage, which was built into the hillside below the house. The house seemed set to view the ranges of mountain peaks that piled up in the distance, each paler and farther off than the peaks before it, wave upon wave of mountain peaks into the hazy horizon.

Shari tugged urgently at Peter's hand. They had to get out of sight in case someone was watching them. She drew him off the road, and they squatted behind a stand of weeds. A screen door snapped shut. There stood Mrs. Wallace. Shari had seen her passing by in her truck and once in Mabel's store. She was a stumpy-looking lady with a neat cap of short white hair framing a round, bright face with clear gray eyes that seemed to see great distances. She didn't look that old, Shari thought. Shari liked the straight, capable look the woman had, a no-nonsense look emphasized by the plain clothes Mrs. Wallace wore—jeans and a loose plaid shirt with rolled-up sleeves. But how people looked didn't always tell how they were inside. Charlotte was pretty, and BeeJay's rubbery mouth gave a humorous impression, but neither of them could be trusted.

At first, it seemed the swallows darting from their mud nests along the eaves of Mrs. Wallace's roof and swooping down over her head might be trying to protect their territory. Then Shari realized from the playful way they looped around the front lawn and wheeled back to Mrs. Wallace on the porch again, like dancers skimming the air, that they were greeting a friend. Mrs. Wallace proceeded briskly down the steps to the garage under her house and disappeared from view.

"Is she going away?" Peter whispered.

"I don't know."

"Can you tell anything yet?"

"Not yet. Let's move farther along so we can see the side and backyard." She let Peter lead the way. He crawled under the trailing branches of a spruce, and Shari followed into the evergreen cave.

Mrs. Wallace had only lived up here for three or four years, but had owned this property for much longer. She and her husband had built her house before he died. Shari knew that and also that Mabel was Mrs. Wallace's friend, her only friend in town because Mrs. Wallace wasn't a churchgoer and didn't associate much with anybody else. "Probably thinks she's too good for us country folk," Charlotte said when Lina had wondered aloud why Mrs. Wallace didn't attend church. Neither of Shari's parents were churchgoers either.

"She likes to keep to herself," Lina had said, "but she acts regular enough, not crazy or nothing, I mean."

When Mrs. Wallace emerged from the garage with a

forty-pound bag of birdseed in a wheelbarrow, Shari's heart beat faster. Mrs. Wallace began filling bird feeders. Two wee gray-crested birds with pale, round breasts promptly arrived to feast at the window-shelf feeder, and a noisy blue jay chased a trio of black-capped chickadees who were doing gymnastics about the large feeder on a post.

"Scat, you bully," Mrs. Wallace told the blue jay. It ignored the scolding but kept an eye cocked at her as it gobbled up sunflower seeds. "Think just because you're handsome that I'd invite the likes of you to dinner?" Mrs. Wallace said to the jay. "I don't like your manners." She waved a branch at the jay, which removed itself to a nearby tree.

"Who's she talking to?" Peter whispered.

"She doesn't like blue jays. I don't either," Shari said. "They're mean to other birds."

Mrs. Wallace turned the corner of her house, and suddenly Shari heard a rush of feathers and Mrs. Wallace's voice, soothing now. "Seems you're feeling better, fellow. And you're certainly looking proud this morning. Shall we see what you can do on your own? Shall we try that wing out on the wind today?"

"Come on," Peter whispered, with his hand cupped to Shari's ear. He walked boldly into the open and ducked back into the woods, hiding where the far corner of the house was visible. Hesitantly, Shari followed his lead. She crouched next to him, but all she could see was a caterpillar eating its way through a leaf in front of her nose.

"She's got a big bird in a cage," Peter whispered and moved aside so that Shari could trade places with him.

Hawk! Shari thought, and her heart squeezed with

excitement as she saw the large cage made out of an old rabbit hutch, and the angular-headed bird with the curved beak. It was not much bigger than a robin, but by its beautiful speckled breast and rusty-colored back and tail, she knew it was a sparrow hawk. Mrs. Wallace was reaching into the cage with a leather gardening glove on her hand. She tossed in something grasshopper sized that the hawk struck at and swallowed. It lifted its wings slightly as it moved on its board perch. The perch was fixed to a broom handle stuck through the cage wires with the ragged-edged broom still attached. The sparrow hawk kept dipping its tail as if to keep its balance, and Mrs. Wallace continued to toss the contents of a plastic bag, piece by piece, into its cage.

"That should hold you for a while," Mrs. Wallace said, and then asked the bird: "Well, what do you say? Is today the day? You can fly back for a handout tomorrow if you need to." She stood aside, leaving the cage door open. The hawk looked around, head tensed. It jumped to the doorway and without hesitation leaped into the air with pointed wings stretched wide and laser eyes intent on freedom. A few flaps of its wings and the hawk had crossed the yard and disappeared into the woods where they dropped away down the mountainside.

Mrs. Wallace waited as if she expected more. She drew off her glove and chewed at the edge of her thumb. Peter stirred restlessly and slapped at a mosquito. A minute passed slowly before anything happened.

"Look," Shari whispered as the hawk flew up out of the woods. Rising swiftly, it gained height until it no longer needed to beat down on the air but could float on the currents gracefully, a black silhouette the shape of a giant swallow against the high blue heavens. It circled overhead higher and higher until at last it was out of sight.

"She set him free," Shari whispered reverently. "She fixed him and set him free."

"He won't die in the woods like Chirpy, will he?" Peter asked.

"Not him. He's a hawk, Peter."

"Well, do you think she's nice then?"

"Yes."

"So do you want me to talk to her now?"

"No need."

"Why not?" He began scratching his mosquito bites. She knew his stomach had to be close to empty and considered heading down to Mabel's store and begging lunch.

"Come on," Shari murmured. "We have to sneak out of here without letting her see us."

"But you didn't ask her about the reward."

"I'm not going to."

"You're going to keep the bird?"

"No. I'll leave it by her front door tomorrow morning before she gets up."

"Then how will she know who to give the reward to?"

"I don't want any reward for finding her swan." Shari couldn't explain it better than that, even though Peter looked confused and kept asking her why not.

"Mama will kill you," he warned.

"I don't care. Anyway, maybe Zeke will get home tomorrow, and he won't let her."

As they left, Shari glanced back and saw Mrs. Wallace still standing with fingers pressed into the small of her arched back as she stared at the Presidential Range, which rose in still gray waves beyond the green crests of the nearby mountains. How wonderful, Shari thought, to find a person who liked the same things she did. She hadn't known anyone like herself existed in the world. It was right that the crystal bird should belong to Mrs. Wallace, and if Shari was lucky enough to see her face when she opened her front door and found it on her doorstep, that would be reward enough.

Four

"*Don't think* just because Zeke's coming home that you're getting away with it," Charlotte had warned when she found out what Shari had done with the crystal bird. "I'll teach you you can't do just like you please. Think you can act like what I tell you don't matter? You just wait, Shari Ape Face."

The vague threat was more frightening than the quick slap or pinch, the violent yank on a handful of Shari's long hair. It raised gray images of past punishments—the classmate's birthday party Shari had been kept from attending at the last minute, the doll she had been forced to share with her younger brothers, who ruined it, the garage-sale dress Charlotte had bought two sizes too big and insisted Shari wear on the first day of school last year, and furthest back, before Peter was born, a day spent tied to the leg of a bed while rain drummed on the roof of the empty house.

Shari ventured up from the basement where Charlotte had sent her to sort and fold wash. The living room looked unfamiliar with everything picked up. Uncluttered by discarded clothes and soda cans and books and toys, it looked bare. This morning Charlotte had given them all clean-up assignments and instructed, "Now don't start messing up the place before your father gets home. Be careful you don't miss the toilet bowl, and leave the clean towels alone until tomorrow."

Charlotte's hair was done in a mass of curls, like a young girl's, and she wore a new scoop-necked pink stretch top and lipstick that matched. She kept dashing between the kitchen, where she had an apple pie baking for Zeke's belated birthday celebration, and the front window, where she and Peter were keeping watch.

On Zeke's first day home, Charlotte's game was to treat him like a guest. It was a game they all liked to play, fun until the inevitable moment when Charlotte started telling Zeke all the things "his" kids had done wrong and all the appliances that had failed and the chores that needed doing. Zeke would wince at her change in tone and try to hold her off a while longer. "Now, Charl, I'll take care of it," he would say. "Just relax. I'll get to it eventually." He'd handle the discipline, meting out fair judgments and moderate punishments, and until he left again, the soothing sound of saw and hammer and ax would lull Charlotte. She would relax and be easygoing, even playful, with Zeke. Then the call would come for him to pick up a load of apples or lumber or light fixtures for delivery in Dubuque or Atlanta or Chicago where still other goods awaited shipment back and forth on the highways across America. Sometimes he was gone for only a few days, but often it was weeks.

Shari couldn't remember how it had been when Zeke worked for a meat-packing company in Rutland and came home every night. She had been Peter's age then. When Charlotte spoke of those years with longing, Zeke would say to her, "Come on; get off it, sweetheart. You know we fought all the time. You were always on my back."

"No, I wasn't. How can you say such a thing? I'm no nag," Charlotte would protest.

"Not a nag?" Zeke would laugh. "I bet you'd take first prize in a nagging contest anywhere in the U.S.A." He'd grin when she exploded and cajole her with, "Never mind. You're still my sweet girl. It's okay. I know you got to complain to someone and it might as well be me. All's I'm saying is, we're better off the way things are. And the money's better too, isn't it?"

"Yes," she would agree reluctantly to that, and the discussion would end until the next time.

"He's here!" Peter shrilled. He leaped from his perch on the back of the chair to run to the front door.

Excitement bubbled in the air, and everybody smiled, including Walter and Doug, who had been at their stand and were now hanging out the windows of Zeke's rig. The big cab looked misshapen with its oversized wheels and no trailer behind it. Zeke blew his sonorous horn, announcing his arrival far and wide in the valley. He parked the cab and jumped from it, arms out to receive Charlotte in a swinging hug and a long kiss. Peter hopped impatiently onto his father's broad back, while Zeke swayed Charlotte back and forth in his arms as if he couldn't bear to let go of her. She looked small and girlish against his burly form.

"Glad to see me, honey? Glad to see your old man?" Zeke asked her, grinning.

"You big old bear. You could've shaved." But he never shaved until the morning after he arrived. His ritual was to grow his beard and mustache all the while he was gone and shave it off when he got home.

Now Zeke was dangling Peter from his arm, letting him hang like a side of beef being weighed on a butcher's scale. "You're getting there, fella. Going to be as big as your brothers any day now."

"What'd you bring me?" Peter asked. "Something to eat?" He preferred eating presents, the pecans from Georgia, dates and figs from California and Arizona, fruitcakes from the South. Zeke always brought each of them something. Last time he'd given them geodes from the desert, round stone balls that might have interesting crystals inside or might not. Shari still had hers intact in her room. She couldn't bear to split the gray shell apart in case nothing at all was inside. Once, Zeke had brought her a beaded Indian vest made of deerskin, a marvelous present that made her wonder if her father knew she'd like to have been an Indian. She hadn't gotten around to asking him before Charlotte lent the vest to an acquaintance's daughter to use in a school play. Shari hadn't gotten it back, even though she'd forced herself past her shyness to ask the girl to please return it.

"You're going to mess up my new outfit," Charlotte squealed as Zeke gave her another squeeze.

"Come inside and I'll mess you up some more where the neighbors can't see," Zeke said. And then he remembered Shari. "Where's my little girl? Where's my littlest sweetheart?"

Shari rushed from the doorway, reaching up her arms for his rough hug and kiss. "I'm so glad you're home, Daddy," she said huskily.

"Hey, Dad," Doug said, as they trooped after Zeke into the living room. "There's going to be a carnival this weekend. Could you take us?"

"We'll see. First I got to sleep for about a week to make up for all the time I lost on the road."

"Can I go to the carnival too, Daddy, please? Can I go too?" Peter begged.

"How long will you be home this time?" Charlotte asked him anxiously, and before he had a chance to answer, "You didn't notice my new hair style. Do you like it?"

"It's beautiful, Charl. You're beautiful. You get prettier instead of older."

She giggled and leaned against him, asking, "Glad to see me, honey? Glad to see me after so long on the road?"

"Glad's not the half of it," he told her and caught Peter in a headlock, pretending not to notice as Pete squawked to be let loose.

"Well," Zeke said to Charlotte, "shall I wash up first, or are you going to offer me a beer?"

"I'm going to invite you into the kitchen. We got a surprise for you," she said. She took his arm possessively, tucking hers around his meaty one. "I hope you're hungry."

"Ain't I always?"

With his free hand, he patted Shari's back as if to acknowledge her existence as he let his wife lead him into the kitchen, where balloons were hung from the light fixture and the sweet, cinnamony aroma of apple pie filled the air. The small presents they had bought or made for him were waiting in a pile beside his plate.

"Surprise, surprise. Happy birthday," Charlotte said, echoed in a round by the children.

"Is it my birthday?" Zeke asked.

"You had it last week on the road, but we're celebrating now," Doug patiently explained.

"You know, you're right. I got a whole year older while I wasn't even looking. Imagine that!"

Without being asked, Doug got a beer for his father and opened it. "Can Walt and me have one too, Dad?"

"You kids can have a sip of mine, seeing as this is a celebration," Zeke said and sat down at his place at the table with an exaggerated sigh of satisfaction. "Lord, it is *good* to be home," he said. Immediately Peter clamored for his father to open his presents, but Zeke wasn't to be rushed. He liked to sniff at things and shake them and guess until his family was wild with the suspense, even though they knew well enough what was inside each package. Charlotte had bought him a new windbreaker to replace the one he'd left at a diner somewhere. Walter and Doug had chipped in for ammunition for his deer-hunting rifle. Peter had bought a cigar, even though Zeke didn't smoke. Shari's gift was chocolate fudge she'd made herself.

"Sweets from my little girl," Zeke said. "What could be better?"

"You know what your sweet little girl went and did?" Charlotte asked irritably, breaking her truce day for the first time ever. They hadn't finished the birthday celebration; they hadn't even gotten to her apple pie. "You know what she did?" Charlotte repeated, without looking at Shari who was quivering at this unexpected outbreak of her mother's fury.

"Do you really want to tell me now?" Zeke asked with a flatness that revealed his lack of enthusiasm for hearing what Shari had done.

"Well, it'll keep you from acting like a fool being nice to this stuck-up kid who thinks she's too good to pick up easy money when she gets the chance. Thinks we're rich or something."

"She is rich," Zeke said. "She's got everything she needs including a loving family, don't she?"

"A little extra money never hurts," Charlotte said. "Anyway, why are you defending her right off before you hear what happened?"

"And why are you starting in before I've had a chance to relax and get acquainted with my family again. Or do you only want me home to hear your complaints?"

His anger deflated Charlotte instantly. She seemed to shrink as she stood at the stove, and her voice was thin as she asked him, "You want your steak well done like usual?"

Now it was his turn to gear down. "Let's not fight, Charl," he begged. "Let's just—"

She flashed her eyes at him. "Always what *you* need. Think it's so easy being alone here with these kids night and day for weeks on end? Think I got it so good?"

Zeke sighed and finished his beer in two gulps.

"Okay," he said to his daughter. "How'd you lose us a fortune, Shari baby?"

Tonelessly she told him. "I found something, and Mama thought I could get a reward for it, but I returned it to the lady and didn't ask her for anything. Mama said I had to return it. She said it belonged to Mrs. Wallace."

"What was it?"

"Just a glass bird. It was really pretty."

"It was crystal. I saw something like it that cost a small fortune in the fancy gift shop in the mall," Charlotte added.

"And what'd Mrs. Wallace say when you gave it back to her, Shari?" Zeke asked.

Shari hung her head. "Nothing—to me. I just left it on her steps this morning and hid in the woods until she came outside."

"Why'd you wait?"

"To see her face. She looked happy, Daddy. And I heard her say, 'Oh, my, how on earth did this get back here?'"

"But you were too shy to talk to her."

Shari shrugged and didn't correct him. It was true being shy had been part of it. The rest was a sense that it would taint the charm of the bird to demand money for returning it to its rightful owner. She wished she had the words to make Zeke understand.

"Shy my eye," Charlotte said. "She was just out to spite me. She just refuses no matter what I ask her. You think she's so sweet, but you don't see what she's like when you're not around."

"I do everything you tell me," Shari was stung into protesting. "I do everything you say."

"All right now," Zeke said. "If this is how it's going to go, I'm calling the dispatch office and getting the next load out of here. No way am I going to tolerate all this scrapping."

"Then why don't you tell that kid to shut her face?" Charlotte yelled, no longer pretty now that she was bulging red with outrage. "Whose side are you on, mine or the kids'? You come home after drinking beer all around the country with your road buddies and won't even back me up. You leave me to deal with these kids who are always into something and won't listen. Think it's fun, living here alone in this rat-hole town?"

The homecoming celebration had ended so abruptly that they never got to eat the apple pie. Zeke concentrated on calming Charlotte down and petting her back into good temper. He told her she was his darling, and, of course, he understood how hard she had it with him gone all the time, and she was a wonderful, brave woman, and didn't she want to see the trinket he'd brought her? Wouldn't she come upstairs with him? The kids could do the dishes. He'd visit with them tomorrow.

Neither parent had come downstairs again. Doug fell asleep in front of the television set. Walter settled into a book, his eyes riding steadily back and forth across the pages. Peter kept asking when they were going to eat the pie.

"We can't until Zeke has his piece," Shari said and finally told Peter it was time for him to go to bed. He was half-asleep and crabby as she stood him in front of the toilet and made sure he aimed at the bowl instead of the wall. Then she got him to wash his face and hands and brush his teeth before he rolled into bed in his underpants. She covered him and kissed him good night and went to her own bedroom.

The squeaking of bedsprings and Charlotte's low laugh came through the thin wall of Shari's bedroom. From past experience, Shari knew her parents would be all right in the morning. She wondered, as she lay in bed listening to the night sounds outside, if telling Zeke on her had been enough punishment to satisfy Charlotte, or if more was still coming because Shari had not asked for the reward. It was hard to know with Charlotte. Little things enraged her, yet she'd overlook serious ones altogether.

Maybe after Zeke fixed Charlotte's car and before she put him to work on the septic tank that was beginning to smell in the backyard, Zeke would take them all to the lake for a swim or to the carnival Doug had mentioned. It was always better when Zeke was around. Chances were he wouldn't be angry with Shari, and if she was lucky, she'd get some stray moments alone with him.

Five

For two days Zeke worked on Charlotte's car, replacing a head gasket and correcting the engine's faulty timing, while Shari and Peter hung just back of his elbow. They brought him rags for wiping greasy engine parts and beers for quenching his thirst while he treated the car's ailments.

"Don't think I've finished with you," Charlotte had warned, but Shari didn't let the threat mar her enjoyment of Zeke's good-humored presence, the occasional hug, the back rub with the knuckles of his greasy fingers. In a moment of mischief, when the temperature had hit the nineties and Zeke was raining perspiration even working in the shade of the trees, Shari turned the garden hose on him.

"How about me?" Peter asked promptly, and Zeke laughed as she drenched them both.

"Okay, now this time it's going to work," Zeke announced for the fifth time, after his hose shower. "Start her up, Pete."

They cheered when the engine caught and continued running. "Told you!" Zeke said jubilantly. "Just give me the tools and the time and I can fix it."

"Why don't you open a garage?" Shari said. "Then you could stay home with us all the time." She knew he had worked in a garage before he was married.

"It'd be nice, but it takes money to start something like that, and there's no guarantee I'd make enough from it to keep us in groceries even if I had the money to get started." The garage Zeke had worked in had failed to make a profit and had gone out of business long ago.

"We could be your helpers," Peter said eagerly. "We'd work cheap."

Zeke ruffled Peter's hair and said, "You and Shari sure are good helpers, but I'd better keep the job I have. There's plenty of men in this country would be glad to get my job."

"Zeke," Shari said, taking the hand he offered her as they walked to the house. "What do you have to do to be a flyer? To pilot a jet, I mean?"

"A pilot? Who'd want to do that?"

"Me."

"You?" He stopped and stared at her. "Where'd you get that idea, Shari? Who's been talking to you?"

She flinched from the sudden tension in his voice and pulled her hand from his, even though she couldn't remember the last time Zeke had been angry at her. "It's my own idea. I'd just like to . . . It's just what I want to be, Daddy."

For a minute he studied her. Then he relaxed and said, "Sorry, honey. I didn't mean to scare you. It's just, I knew a feller once who was a pilot. I didn't like him. . . . I guess to fly a big plane you got to take lessons, and it'd cost plenty—more than we've got. I wouldn't count on becoming a pilot if I was you. Why don't you think of something you can do closer to home?"

As they were about to enter the house, Zeke added in a low voice, "Shari, one thing—don't *ever* say anything to your mother about wanting to be a pilot. Okay?"

Shari nodded without asking questions. It was only much later that she remembered Peter had already told Charlotte about her desire to fly. She wondered about the man whom Zeke hadn't liked. Had Charlotte known him too?

At supper that night Zeke announced, "Tomorrow we go to the lake and maybe take in the carnival on the way home. Doug, you put a sign on your vegetable stand that you went fishing. No arguments. You're already the richest twelve-year-old kid in town."

Next morning when Shari came downstairs in her peppermint candy-cane swimsuit that Zeke said made her look delicious, Charlotte said to her, "What are you dressed up for? You're not going with us."

Shari stopped short of the breakfast table. "Why not?"

"I told you I was going to teach you a lesson, didn't I?" Charlotte said. "Next time maybe you'll do what I tell you."

Shari looked over at her father who was crouched over a plate of eggs, head bent nearly to his hairy forearms. "Daddy?" she asked.

He looked at her guiltily and muttered, "This is between you and your mother, Shari. She's the one in charge when I'm on the road. If she wants to punish you for what you done, then I can't interfere."

Without a word, Shari ran back to her room and threw herself down onto her carefully made-up bed. She squeezed the pillow in anger. What had she done that was so terrible? Just because she hadn't asked for a five-dollar reward, Charlotte had deprived her of the summer's best treat. That was so mean, so unfair and rotten—mean! Shari was still shaking with frustration when she heard the car engine's coughing become a steady growl.

When they had gone, the anger whooshed out of her. Zeke had left her behind. She lay listlessly while birds chatted back and forth in the tree outside her window and the silence of the empty house gathered around her. After a while, she took a deep breath and got up. Senseless to lie around indoors on a summer day. Besides, for all she knew, they might have left a message for her.

She went downstairs. Nothing in the kitchen; nothing in the bare yard except Peter's plastic pool, dirty with leaves and twigs and gravel in the few inches of leftover water in the bottom. Peter, at least, should have come to tell her he was sorry she wasn't going with them. He'd gone off without a thought for her. No loyalty in him, either. Of course, he was only six. As for Zeke, she knew that he had to appease Charlotte. Just as well he had. Times past when he'd interfered on Shari's behalf, Charlotte had made her pay double when he wasn't around. Certainly Shari couldn't expect anything from Doug and Walter. Their concern was for each other. They had never cared much about her.

"Don't think," Shari ordered herself out loud. She would not go around feeling wronged. Stupid to make herself feel worse instead of better. The woods were still there for her. Without Peter to hold her back, she could climb and explore new places. She could make the day good for herself instead of lying around and suffering. All of a sudden, a pang of hunger reminded her that she hadn't had breakfast. The first thing to do was eat.

For safety's sake, and because she hated the sound of gunshots, Shari didn't go far into the woods during the fall hunting season. The rest of the year she rarely saw another person during her solitary explorations. It startled her, therefore, to see a stumpy figure in jeans and a loose shirt high up on the mountain, far from any path. Shari hid behind a tree to see without being seen. Hard to tell whether the figure studying the sky through binoculars was male or female, but the cap of white hair gave her away. What was Mrs. Wallace doing climbing around up here, Shari wondered. Did Mrs. Wallace also know the ledge Shari called Eagle's Perch?

She was used to wondering about things that her shyness kept her from investigating, and she would have slipped past unobserved if Mrs. Wallace hadn't gasped, "There he is."

As Mrs. Wallace lifted the binoculars to her eyes again, Shari stepped away from the tree so she could

see out into the valley. Sure enough, it was the eagle.
He had his nest in a bare-armed tree that commanded
the valley and seemed to grow out from the rock ledge.
Now he was resting on the wind high overhead, cir-
cling on magnificent outstretched wings. Shari watched
in awe. She had looked him up in the bird book in the
reference section of the library; so she knew by his size
and the broad, flat, feather-fingered wings that he was
a bald eagle and not a large hawk. Her impulse was to
share her knowledge with Mrs. Wallace.

Mrs. Wallace raised a camera hanging from a leather
strap around her neck and said aloud, "Light's wrong,
darn it." She let go of both binoculars and camera to
simply watch.

It was the moment for Shari to leave, but she waited
until Mrs. Wallace turned and discovered her. "Good
heavens!" Mrs. Wallace said. "For an instant I thought
you were an Indian spirit returning to your old hunting territory. What are you doing up here, child?"

"Climbing."

"All by yourself?"

"Yes."

"Well, I'm glad to know I'm not the only one crazy
enough to go wandering around mountains alone.
Have you seen the eagle?"

"Yes. . . . I know where he nests."

"You do?" Mrs. Wallace looked genuinely impressed.
"Would you believe that's what I climbed all the way up
here to find? His nest. I thought it would interest my
granddaughters if I photographed it for them. Of
course, I'd like a picture of that big handsome bird in
the flesh, or should I say feather, as well. I don't sup-

pose you could call him down and get him to pose for me?"

Shari smiled. "No, but I could show you where the nest is."

"Would you? Is it within reach of an overweight, not so agile older party like me?"

Shari considered. "You could get close enough to take a picture."

"Lead on," Mrs. Wallace said. "What shall I call you?"

"I'm Shari."

"That's a pretty name. I'm Eve Wallace."

"I know."

"You do?"

Shari nodded, too embarrassed to confess her secret observation of Mrs. Wallace at her house.

"I keep forgetting that all the local people seem to know me even when I don't know them. It's an interesting phenomenon for someone like me who isn't used to living in a small town. You are local, aren't you?"

"Yes," Shari said. She didn't offer more information than that, and Mrs. Wallace didn't pry.

Shari walked ahead, holding back branches for Mrs. Wallace and taking the easiest route up to Eagle's Perch.

"You're quite a woodsman," Mrs. Wallace said with admiration when they stopped for her to catch her breath.

"I like the woods," Shari said and pointed to the tree whose thick arm reached out as if in judgment over the valley. In a crook between the two largest branches was the eagle's dishpan-sized nest of brown twigs.

"I owe you one for this," Mrs. Wallace said and promptly set about taking pictures. "My husband used to be the family photographer. This is his camera, much too fancy for a beginner like me, but I'm learning." She snapped pictures from a few different angles before buttoning her camera back into its case.

"Are you a fellow birder, Shari?"

"What?"

"Do you like to watch birds a lot?"

"Oh, yes."

"Seen any interesting ones besides this eagle?"

"I'm not too good at names," Shari said. "I try to look up what I see, but sometimes I forget the markings before I get to the library. I don't get there that often."

"Don't you have a Peterson's field guide?"

"No."

"Would you like one? I've got an extra. Cover's worn, but it's still good."

"Oh, no thank you."

"I'd like to give you something in exchange for showing me that nest."

"You don't have to."

"Tell you what—I'll leave the book at Mabel's store, and you can borrow it, keep it, or return it there as you like. You get to Mabel's store occasionally, don't you?"

"Everybody around here does."

"Yes, that's what I thought. Mabel's a friend of mine."

"I know."

Mrs. Wallace laughed. "It's not fair for you to know

so much about me when I don't know anything about you," she said.

The invitation to talk about herself made Shari uneasy. She dropped her eyes and looked away. She had already had a longer conversation with Mrs. Wallace than she had ever had with an adult at first meeting.

"You know," Mrs. Wallace said, "I'm going to need a guide to get me out of here. I don't have a clue which way to go except down."

"Just follow me," Shari said.

"Can you bring me out close to Mabel's store? That's where I left my car. Mabel's the one who told me about the eagle. My house looks off toward different mountains."

Shari nodded and struck off at a new angle down the mountains, leading Mrs. Wallace toward the Bravermans' land. They wouldn't object to two trespassers in their overgrown back fields, and passage in that direction would be easiest.

"Any time you want a recommendation as a mountain guide, just ask," Mrs. Wallace said when they emerged onto an old wagon road whose ruts were still not filled in with weeds.

"There used to be a house here," Shari said, turning away from the compliment, which pleased her nonetheless. "This is the Bravermans' place. Their grandfather lived here, but the house burned in a fire years ago." The katydids kept up a harsh, monotonous ratcheting in the tough field grass around them. "See there." Shari pointed at the roofless building whose front door hung open at a drunken angle revealing a steep flight of stairs.

"Moo," a cow lowed plaintively. *"Mooooooo."*

Suddenly, three blond heads appeared around a blackberry patch that had hidden them. "There she goes again, Sue Ellen," a shrill voice piped. "She's around here somewheres."

"In the house, Sue Ellen?" a girl identical to the first blond eight-year-old suggested.

"That old cow'd never fit through the front door," Sue Ellen said. Then she set her hands on her plump hips as she stared through the gaping entrance at the steep center hall steps and said, "Well, I'll be! Look where that fool cow got to!"

The three Braverman girls hadn't noticed Shari and Mrs. Wallace because the blackberry patch had separated them, and when Mrs. Wallace called out, "Need any help?" Shari shrank back out of sight. She and Sue Ellen had been friends once, but no more. Despite Sue Ellen's womanly curves, she was thirteen and in the same grade as Shari at school.

"What's the matter, Shari?" Mrs. Wallace asked in a voice too low for Sue Ellen to hear. "Don't you want to help them?"

Since she saw no way out of it, Shari followed Mrs. Wallace over to the roofless house. Sue Ellen's eyes narrowed suspiciously when she saw Shari coming. "What are *you* doing around here?" Sue Ellen asked.

"Shari was guiding me back to the road," Mrs. Wallace said pleasantly. "What can we do for you?"

"Fool cow got herself up the stairs somehow, and now she don't know how to get down." They stood and surveyed the situation. The cow stood facing them at the top of the steps. Every once in a while it opened its big mouth to moo in distress. Its broad black-and-white face and pitiful expression were so ridiculous that Mrs. Wallace grinned, and Shari found herself smiling too.

"It's not funny," Sue Ellen said sharply. "That's an expensive cow. She could break a leg on them stairs."

"You're right. I'm sorry," Mrs. Wallace said and got rid of all the laughter on her face except for the twinkle in her eyes.

Again Mrs. Wallace offered assistance.

"You could go tell my mother to call my father or the fire department," Sue Ellen said ungraciously. "We'll never get that cow out of here by ourselves."

"Right," Mrs. Wallace said. "Shari, do you know the way to this girl's house?"

"Sure she knows it," Sue Ellen said.

Shari turned in silence and began hurrying through the rusted farm machinery and broken bottles to the pasture. The downed, barbed-wire fence there explained the cow's escape route. When the bawling of the animal had diminished behind them, Mrs. Wallace asked, "Is that girl a friend of yours, Shari?"

"Not anymore," Shari said. Again, Mrs. Wallace failed to pry. They hiked across the pasture, lumpy with tufts of grass, rocks and juniper bushes, toward the distant farmhouse.

It was too long and complicated a story to tell, Shari thought. Her relationship to Sue Ellen Braverman began way back when Charlotte and Sue Ellen's mother became girlhood enemies. "That woman's a gossip and a busybody," Charlotte had told Shari, "and don't you have anything to do with her daughter. I don't care if she's the only kid around here your age. I don't ever

want her in this house and don't you go near hers neither."

Nevertheless, one day at recess in first grade, Sue
Ellen had said sensibly to Shari, "Listen, just 'cause our
mamas don't like each other don't mean we can't be
friends. Let's us be friends, Shari. Don't no one but us
have to know about it."

Shari had warmed instantly to the idea of a secret
friendship, and she'd been faithful to Sue Ellen in
school and out, meeting her sometimes in Sue Ellen's
grandfather's house to talk through sweet stolen hours
of an afternoon. No matter that Shari hadn't been interested in the things Sue Ellen cared about. Listening
had connected Shari to that larger world to which Sue
Ellen belonged and given her the satisfaction of knowing she had a friend. By third grade, Sue Ellen had
already added boys to her endless chatter about clothes
and who said what mean thing to whom. She liked to
elaborate on her dreams of getting married and having
babies and owning a four-poster bed and an in-ground
swimming pool. Her only requirement of Shari was
that she listen. Then one day, Sue Ellen noticed black-
and-blue marks on Shari's arms.

"I bet it was Zeke done it," Sue Ellen said. At Shari's
horrified denial, Sue Ellen had guessed, "Charlotte,
then. It was your mother, wasn't it?"

"Don't tell anybody," Shari had gasped, and Sue
Ellen had promised solemnly that her lips were sealed.

A few days later Shari discovered that every girl in
her class was aware that her mother had beaten her.
Sue Ellen was a person to avoid, not a friend at all.

For a while Sue Ellen acted as if she didn't care that
their friendship had ended. She had become friends

with an older girl who had moved in nearby and no longer needed Shari anyway. After the older girl left town, Sue Ellen did try to renew her friendship with Shari, but when Shari remained cool to her, they became enemies. They were enemies still.

Mrs. Wallace reported the plight of the cow to Mrs. Braverman while Shari waited outside. The two of them resumed their progress toward the road. "It *was* a funny sight though, wasn't it?" Mrs. Wallace said. "That cow looked so bewildered. Too bad we can't see how they get her down those stairs."

"I wonder what made her climb up them," Shari said.

"Curiosity?" Mrs. Wallace suggested.

"A cow?"

"I guess not. Although I suspect most creatures have some curiosity in them. Anyway, I can see why that girl's not your friend. She's about as charming as the prickers on a blackberry vine."

Shari laughed and didn't deny it. She refused Mrs. Wallace's offer to buy her a soda or ice cream when they got to Mabel's store though, saying she had to get home. It was the truth.

"Well, Shari, you made my day," Mrs. Wallace said. "I'll send you that bird guide via Mabel, and if you should ever get a chance to stop in to see me, I hope you will."

Shari nodded, waved and hurried off. She knew Mrs. Wallace was just being polite. It would be nice to visit her, but Shari didn't expect she ever would.

That night Peter brought Shari his unopened bag of potato chips and a candy bar, gifts of love from a boy who treasured food as much as he did. Immediately, she forgave him. "I had a good day too," she told him. "I climbed all the way to Eagle's Perch."

"You went without me?" he asked, as if it were she who had deserted him.

The next day it rained, and Zeke took them to Rutland where Charlotte went shopping for school clothes for them. While she was picking out shirts with the boys, Zeke walked Shari over to the girls' department. "Anything you want, honey. You pick it out and I'll pay for it," he said.

He was trying to make up for leaving her out of yesterday's fun, and she didn't want to hurt his feelings, but she'd never cared what she wore and had always been content to let Charlotte pick her clothes, with the exception of the too-big garage-sale dress in which Shari had felt so ugly.

"Mother will get me stuff," Shari said, looking around at the bewildering array of blouses and shirts and pants and dresses and skirts. How did anyone know where to start?

Zeke looked puzzled. "I want to get you something special," he urged.

Shari squeezed his hand. "All I really want's a bird," she said. "And I know you can't get me that."

"I could, Shari, but I'd be in big trouble with your ma if I did."

"I know. It's all right."

"Tell you what. I'll see if I can find something extra special for you next trip," he promised.

Another vest as pretty as the beaded Indian one that he'd brought her that Charlotte had given away? But Shari would never wear anything that unusual now.

The last thing she wanted was to make herself stand out from the other girls.

"I don't need anything," she said. "I'm fine, Daddy."

"You're a good girl," he said, "the best any father could have."

She liked the compliment better than anything he could have bought her. It made a happy glow inside her all afternoon.

Six

The day before Zeke was going back on the road, he came into the kitchen for lunch and announced jovially, "Looks like Shari's getting a reward for returning that lady's property after all."

"What do you mean?" Charlotte asked. She was cutting up celery for the tuna-fish salad.

"Well, when I stopped at the store to pick up your cigarettes, Mabel told me Mrs. Wallace left a box there for Shari."

"Did you bring it?" Charlotte asked.

"No. You know Mabel. She's got her own way of doing things. She wants Shari to come get her gift herself."

"Can I go with you, Shari?" Peter asked and licked off his milk mustache in readiness.

"Sure you can."

Shari nibbled around and around her tuna-fish sandwich, leaving the soft, soggy center for last while she tried to figure out how Mrs. Wallace could have found out who had returned her crystal swan. The fact that Mrs. Wallace had gotten her a gift wasn't surprising. It was the kind of thing she herself would have done if their positions were reversed.

Peter jiggled with excitement as they walked the quarter mile to the store. "I hope it's something to eat," he said.

"Maybe it's a box of candy," Shari said smiling. They swung their clasped hands in rhythm with their steps as they walked along the gravelly verge of the road out of the way of the cars swishing by. They passed Horner's farm with its big red barn and muddy yard and toy-sized cows pasted on the distant hillside field. Woods came next and then the small, square, white Pentecostal church with a black-lettered sign out front announcing Sunday services. The minister's topic was to be, "Leading the black sheep back to the fold." The duck pond was empty for a change, which meant the ducks had been carried off to market, still quacking, in slatted crates.

Across the way was Mabel's store with its gas pump and saggy wooden porch decorated with cartons of empty soda bottles and an unopened crate of melons. "Vermont cheese" read the handwritten sign on one side of the glass-windowed front door; "Vermont maple syrup" read the sign on the other.

Mabel sold what was labeled penny candy from open glass jars on her counter, but she charged five cents a piece, or whatever she felt like that day. Sometimes she gave candy away free. Or she would bend her thin overalled length, extended by one of her pairs of dangling earrings, over the barrel of sunflower seeds and dip out a free bagful for Shari to feed to the birds. Mabel liked children. Her active, three-year-old grandson used the narrow aisles of the small store as roadways for his trucks. Unwary shoppers were warned by Mabel to watch out that they didn't get run over.

"There you are!" Mabel called as soon as Shari stepped into the dim, cheesey-smelling interior. "Told your father to send you down here in a hurry. Look what was left here for you this morning!" She sounded as excited as if the surprise were for her as she handed Shari a small cardboard box with air holes. "Be careful how you peek inside, now. You don't want to let what's in there out."

"A bird," Shari said, unbelieving even as she lifted a corner of the top and peered in the box. "A blue parakeet!" Joy flooded her.

"Pretty little fella, ain't he?" Mabel leaned on the counter companionably.

"He's beautiful. He's the bluest blue. He's—beautiful." Shari, who rarely cried, found herself choking with tears.

Mabel cracked the gum she was chewing. "Tickled pink, just like I thought she'd be," she said smugly.

"Let me see," Peter demanded. Shari held the box carefully to allow him to look inside.

"How did Mrs. Wallace know?" she asked.

"That you wanted a bird? Well, she asked me to find out what you'd like, so I asked Zeke, and he said a bird. He said your ma might not be too thrilled, but he thought she'd probably let you keep it once you got it."

"But how did Mrs. Wallace know it was me gave her back the crystal swan?" Shari asked.

"Oh, that was your ma. She come in here one morning and said how you'd returned the thing and been too shy to say anything. She said she thought you was owed a reward."

Suddenly Shari saw how it had worked out. Charlotte had done her a favor without meaning to, and Zeke had taken a chance for her sake. This time life hadn't been unfair, just tricky.

The bird scrabbled around in the box. "Let's get him home and let him out of there," Peter said. "Do you think Mama will let you keep him?"

"I don't know," Shari said, unwilling to consider any possible negatives.

Mabel insisted on closing her store and driving Shari and Peter and the bird home, even though Shari assured her that walking was no problem. "I'll go in with you in case your mother wants to know who to blame," Mabel said.

"Blame?" Peter asked. "What for?"

"With your ma, you can never tell," Mabel said.

She pulled her car up in their driveway and followed Shari and Peter to the kitchen door. "Yoo hoo," she called. "Charlotte, come see what Eve Wallace got Shari as a reward."

"It's a parakeet, Mama," Peter said. "He's blue with a white head and a black ring around his eye."

Charlotte stood in the doorway with a lit cigarette in her mouth. She took a puff, staring at the box, and asked, "What kind of reward is that?"

"A good one for a girl who likes birds," Mabel said.

"And who told Mrs. Wallace Shari likes birds?"

"I guess it must've been me," Mabel said thoughtfully. "I remember Shari was always coming in for birdseed last year, and didn't *you* tell me how bad she felt when it died on her?"

"She left the window open, and it flew away," Charlotte said.

"Is that what happened? Well, I'm sure she'll take better care of this little fella," Mabel said cheerfully. "Anyway a bird's no trouble, and Shari's a year older and wiser."

Charlotte frowned at the box and said nothing.

Mabel grinned and winked at Shari. "I'll tell Eve Wallace how pleased you are."

"I'm going to thank her myself," Shari said.

"Good idea. Want a lift up there tomorrow afternoon? Her and I usually visit Thursday afternoons when my Charley takes over the store for me."

"I don't need a ride, but thank you for the offer, Mabel."

"You're not gonna *walk* that far? It's got to be three or four miles, child," Mabel objected.

"Not the way I go. I know a shortcut."

"Well, suit yourself."

Mabel explained to Charlotte that Mrs. Wallace had also paid for a year's worth of birdseed and gravel as part of her gift to Shari. "Ain't that nice?"

"Mmmmmm." Charlotte's eyes narrowed as she took short, quick puffs on her cigarette.

When Mabel drove off with a farewell toot of her horn, Shari looked straight at her mother and said, "Thank you very much."

"For what?"

"For not making me give back the bird."

"Why would I do that? Just be sure it doesn't make a mess in your room. And this time, keep your window shut."

Shari didn't say anything. She wondered if Charlotte could truly have forgotten who opened that window last summer.

Peter closed Shari's bedroom door and Shari made sure the screen on her window was latched before she transferred the bird to the old cage that had stood empty all year. She filled the water and feeder cups and lined the cage with notebook paper, while the parakeet huddled fearfully on a dowel perch in the cage with its feathers fluffed out.

"What are you going to call him?" Peter asked.

"Blue Boy," Shari said without hesitation.

"I thought it was Zeke told Mabel you wanted a bird," Peter said while they waited for Blue Boy to adjust to his new environment. "But Mabel didn't say it that way to Mama. Mabel said *she* was the one told Mrs. Wallace you—"

"What's the difference?" Shari asked. "As long as I can keep Blue Boy, that's all that matters."

"But why did Mabel tell us it was Daddy told her and tell Mama different?"

"Peter," Shari said earnestly, "don't talk about it, huh? And if you want to play with Blue Boy, be sure you don't leave my door or window open so he can fly out of this room."

"You don't have to tell me that," he said. "Think I'm dumb or something?"

Just then Blue Boy jumped to the swing in the center of the cage and rocked gently back and forth. He ducked his head and chirped throatily. Then he began to cluck and squawk as if he were talking out his version of his day's adventures. Shari watched him blissfully.

Peter got bored and left her alone with her bird long before Blue Boy had drunk from his water cup, scattered seed from his feeder all over and made a watery gray-and-white deposit on the floor of his cage. She poked a finger through the bars to offer him as a perch, and he pecked at her, but gently. The afternoon sailed by, and suddenly Charlotte was calling her to come down and help get supper ready.

The next morning, Blue Boy sat on Shari's finger, his wiry claws clasped around it, as she promised to buy him a cuttlebone and repeated his name over and over, telling him what a pretty, pretty Blue Boy he was.

"Happy with your bird?" Zeke asked her when she ran downstairs to say goodbye to him.

"Yes," she told him as she kissed his clean-shaven face, although the sight of his packed bag near the door brought on the lurch of despair she usually felt when it was time for him to leave again. Charlotte clung to him and cried as she always did. Doug and Walter had already gone to their stand for the day.

"Come back soon, Daddy, and bring me some choco-late-chip cookies this time," Peter said.

They waved goodbye as Zeke's big cab backed out of the driveway and onto the road heading for the furniture factory where he was to pick up his next load.

Charlotte wiped her eyes and headed for the telephone to wring some comfort from her friends. "You kids stay out of my hair today," she said over her shoulder.

Already the sun was hot, even though it was still morning. No clouds to mar the purity of sky above the basking mountains. "I'm going to visit Mrs. Wallace and thank her," Shari told Peter. "Do you want to stay here with Mama or come with me?"

"Mama told you to call Mrs. Wallace up and thank her when she sent you the bird book. Only you didn't," Peter said. "You could call her now and thank her twice and we wouldn't have to hike all that way."

"If you don't want to come, stay home then," Shari said.

"You're not afraid to use the phone, are you, Shari? Mama said you were afraid to use the phone."

"I don't like to use it," Shari admitted.

"Why not? I don't mind," Peter said.

"I just don't like to," Shari said and tried to explain. "You can't see what people are thinking on the telephone. It's only their voice from a machine. . . . Anyway, you should meet Mrs. Wallace, Peter. She's a nice lady."

"You just like her because she likes birds."

"Mabel says she makes her own jam and bread too," Shari coaxed.

"Will she give us some?" Peter sounded more interested.

"I don't know, and don't you embarrass me by asking her."

"I wouldn't do that," Peter said. "I'm not such a baby."

Once they were through the ravine, the road to Mrs. Wallace's seemed shorter than it had the last time Shari had walked it with Peter. They found Mrs. Wallace weeding her vegetable garden. She looked up when

Shari called hello and said, "Shari! How nice that you came. I was just thinking about you."

"This is Peter, my little brother," Shari said.

"And how are you on this hot summer morning, Peter?" Mrs. Wallace asked.

"Thirsty," Peter said promptly.

"Peter!" Shari scolded.

"I didn't ask. I just answered," Peter said.

At that, Mrs. Wallace laughed so heartily that tears came to her eyes. "Let's go inside for an iced-tea break," she said when she could talk again. "It's too hot to weed all this lettuce anyway. I should have mulched it better. . . . Do butter cookies and lemonade sound good to you, Peter?"

"Yeah!" he said with enthusiasm and glanced at Shari to see if she disapproved.

"Peter likes to eat," Shari said apologetically.

"Nothing wrong with that," Mrs. Wallace said. "I'm very fond of good food myself." She led them into a kitchen so crosshatched with sunlight that the details faded into the brightness. Shari saw plants and hanging pots and onions on a string hooked to an overhead beam. A staircase with a sinewy handrail made of polished tree branches ran up one side of the room. On the other side of the stairs was a red brick wall. Mrs. Wallace gave Shari the job of squeezing the lemons, while Peter was set to placing cookies from the jar onto a plate.

"I came to say thank you," Shari said. "For the beautiful bird and for lending me the bird book."

"It's not a loan," Mrs. Wallace said. "You may keep the book, and I'm glad you like the bird. What did you name him?"

"Blue Boy," Shari said.

"Nice name. I hope he gives you as much pleasure as you gave me by returning that crystal swan. It was one of the last gifts from my husband, and I treasured it especially."

"It's beautiful," Shari said.

Mrs. Wallace helped herself to a cookie and offered Shari iced tea. Shari asked if she could try the lemonade that Peter was having instead.

"It's good," Peter said. "Better than from the can."

"And are you a bird lover like your sister and me, Peter?" Mrs. Wallace asked.

"No, I like trucks," he said.

"Peter wants to be a truck driver like our father," Shari said.

"Or I could get a hamburger stand maybe," Peter offered.

"And eat up all your own hamburgers?" Mrs. Wallace asked.

"Not all. Some of them I'd sell."

Mrs. Wallace smiled. "Shari, you know what I've been thinking about? Do you know anything about bird banding?"

"Is it something to do with keeping track of migrating birds?"

"Yes, and a way of keeping a rough census on the various kinds of birds and their life spans. Banding has lots of purposes. You need to get a license from the U.S. Fish and Wildlife Service first, and then, if you're on a migratory route as we are here, you can set up nets in the spring and fall to catch the birds just long enough to clamp little metal tags on one of their legs.

"Of course, it's important to keep good records.

Eventually, the information is recorded on a central computer and used for the preservation of birds and their environments. It's a big responsibility to be an official bird bander, and if I start, I'd need to keep at it. I'm not sure I could handle it by myself."

"Could I help you?" Shari asked. "I mean, if there's something I could do—"

"I was hoping you'd say that." Mrs. Wallace looked happy.

"Is it a job? Are you going to pay her?" Peter asked.

"Well, it's a job, but the volunteer kind, Peter," Mrs. Wallace said. "People don't usually get paid for bird banding. Although I could give Shari—"

"No, no," Shari said. "I wouldn't want to get paid. It would be fun for me."

"Why do you want to work without getting paid?" Peter asked. "Doug wouldn't, and Mama says it's stupid to work for nothing, like she does in the house."

"Mama doesn't work for nothing. She works to raise us and please Zeke, and Zeke takes care of her and loves her in return."

"Actually, working for love is better than working for money," Mrs. Wallace told Peter. "It's more satisfying to a person."

"I don't get it," Peter said.

"Well, let's see if I can explain it," Mrs. Wallace said. "Lots of important jobs are done for free just because people want to do them. Take people who visit patients in hospitals to cheer them up, and garden-club ladies who beautify their towns with flowers, and volunteers who pile up sandbags to keep rivers from flooding. Lots of things that make life better society can't afford to pay for. Raising children is another good example."

"But if you don't get paid, you won't get any money," Peter argued. "And Doug says you got to have a lot of money to live good."

Mrs. Wallace looked amused. "Well, most people don't spend *all* their time on volunteer activities," she said, "just whatever time they can afford."

"Shari can't afford any. She can't even afford to go to school and be a pilot," Peter said.

"Is that your ambition, Shari?" Mrs. Wallace asked.

"She wants to fly a jet plane," Peter said.

"My father told me you have to go to school to be a pilot," Shari said, looking at Mrs. Wallace for confirmation.

"It's true you need training," Mrs. Wallace said. "But I believe if you join one of the services, like the air force, they'll send you to school and train you, so long as you're physically and mentally capable of doing the job."

"And you don't have to pay for it?"

"Not if you enlist. I think they require you to serve a certain number of years in exchange for your education. Of course, the danger is if there's a war—"

"But you could really be a pilot without having any money?" Shari interrupted eagerly.

"I believe so," Mrs. Wallace said.

Shari's smile stretched out her cheeks.

"She didn't know that," Peter explained unnecessarily, and grandly told his sister, "I guess you might as well help Mrs. Wallace band the birds, Shari, if you don't need to earn no money."

"Thanks, Pete," she said. "I'm glad you approve."

She was teasing, but he nodded, taking her seriously. "I do," he said.

"Well, we'll talk about the bird banding some more once I investigate it a little further and see what we're getting into," Mrs. Wallace said. "It would be nice to have an excuse to see more of you, Shari."

"And me too?" Peter asked.

"The cookie jar will always be out for you, my friend," Mrs. Wallace promised solemnly. Shari laughed, but Peter looked pleased.

It was only a few days later that Charlotte told Shari Mrs. Wallace had called. "She said she wanted to talk to you about some project with birds you and her are going to do together. She said she got a mess of material from the government and she wants to know how much time you're gonna have once school starts. I told her you got no time to go running around after birds. You got plenty to do here for me, and you don't do half of what you should as is."

"I can just go when you don't need me," Shari said.

"Yeah, well, if you want to spend your free time with that crazy lady—"

"She's not crazy."

"No? Going around catching birds and putting bands on their legs sounds crazy to me."

"But it's okay if I go to talk to her about it, isn't it?"

"You want to go climbing around in this heat, go ahead. Just be sure you and your brother stay out of my hair. After I clean out the refrigerator, I've got a pile of mending to do, and Doug's pants need letting out again."

Peter was playing outside when Shari went to ask him if he wanted to go along with her to Mrs. Wallace's.

"It's too hot to walk all that way," Peter said. "I want to play cement mixer in the pool with my trucks."

"All right then. I'll be back later."

Today Shari was glad to leave without him and hurried off before he had a chance to change his mind. She could move faster alone.

The heat brought out the green leafy scent of the woods. Shari breathed deeply of it as she slipped through the lacy sun and shadows under the trees, down into the cool damp of the ravine where the stream burbled slowly over the rocks and even the rapids' roar seemed muted. Up the steep far side, over the projecting ledge—in no time, she had arrived breathless at the edge of Mrs. Wallace's lawn. Shari halted there, locked tight in a fit of shyness by the sight of Mrs. Wallace sitting on her front steps shelling peas.

The head with the neat, white cap of hair lifted and wise eyes found Shari. Mrs. Wallace's round cheeks puffed up in a smile as she said, "There's my young friend. Come sit beside me here in the shade while I finish shelling these peas."

"May I help?"

"You certainly may. Shelling peas is dull work to do alone," Mrs. Wallace said.

Shari relaxed in the warmth of Mrs. Wallace's welcome. She broke a pod into the colander of peas on the stone step between Mrs. Wallace's ample hip and her own slim one, thinking how much she liked this lady.

"I don't know why I grow so many peas," Mrs. Wallace said. "Certainly can't eat them all, and it's a shame to waste them. How about doing me a favor and taking some home to your family?"

"Oh, no thank you," Shari responded with her usual

reluctance to take gifts from someone she didn't know very well. Accepting gifts from strangers was taking charity, Charlotte and Zeke had taught her, unless you had something to give in exchange. "My mother said you wanted to talk to me about the bird banding."

"Your mother didn't sound too enthused about our project."

"She isn't. She thinks birds aren't worth wasting my time on."

"My good friend Mabel would agree. Mabel says it takes a pair of odd ducks like you and me to get more pleasure out of feathered creatures than our own two-legged kind." Mrs. Wallace's lips quirked with a held-back grin. "That's Mabel for you. She thinks I'm in danger of becoming a hermit. I expect you're too young for her to accuse you of that yet."

"What's wrong with hermits?" Shari asked.

"Nothing. I've met ones as nice or nicer than other people, just not as social."

"I watched you before I returned your swan," Shari confessed. "I saw you let that sparrow hawk go."

"Did you?"

"It was wonderful," Shari said with feeling.

Mrs. Wallace's clear gray eyes lit in a smile. "Letting wild creatures go free when they can take care of themselves is an act of respect. I found that hawk flopping around the woods with one damaged wing and fed him for the couple of weeks it took him to heal. That's all. It was beautiful, wasn't it, the way he circled up at the top of the sky as if he never planned to come back down?"

"I like hawks best," Shari said, and hastened to add in case she'd insulted Mrs. Wallace, "I mean, to watch outdoors. Inside I like parakeets. . . . I don't think Blue Boy minds being caged too much."

"Probably not. Anyway, a tropical bird like him would never survive a northern winter outside. That's for sure."

"I had another parakeet. He flew out of my bedroom window last summer and he never came back. I suppose—" She swallowed and left her sentence trembling between them. It was tempting to tell Mrs. Wallace things. She listened patiently as if she cared. Shari had the feeling that Mrs. Wallace would understand even those closed-box secrets she'd hidden from herself, but she couldn't risk letting them out even so. Who knew what monstrous forms they had taken back there in the dark attic of her mind!

"What I need," Shari said dreamily, "is to be a bird or, anyway, some kind of flyer so I can leave the earth behind like the sparrow hawk did."

"You don't find the earth beautiful enough to hold you?"

Shari shrugged. "It's beautiful; it's just that I need to get away from it sometimes."

"What do you need to get away from particularly?"

"Things," Shari said and was relieved when Mrs. Wallace didn't press her further.

"As to wanting to be a bird—" Mrs. Wallace paused to consider it. "There you and I differ. A bird's wings could never provide me with half the adventure my human mind gets from reading and learning and thinking. A bird can only explore the visible world, at least so far as we know, but our minds can go where no creatures have ever been and into the past and on to the future." Mrs. Wallace's smile lifted all the curves of her plain face. "Now how about some lemonade to wash down that heavy dose of philosophy?" she said.

After the lemonade, Mrs. Wallace had to show Shari the oriole's nest hanging like a small, round mailbag from a branch of the cherry tree. Next she told Shari the saga of the tiny wrens who'd chased the larger sparrows away from a birdhouse in which the wrens had nested the year before. "They won out, those little wrens, just by sheer force of character," Mrs. Wallace said.

She told Shari about her granddaughters, Christine and Jackie, and how Jackie was away at soccer camp because she hoped to be a professional ball player when she grew up, and Chris had a job as a mother's helper this year. "I expect to see them in the fall," Mrs. Wallace said, "but I do miss their summer visit. The truth is, I enjoy young people more than adults, except for Mabel."

"I never knew my grandparents," Shari said. "They died in a car crash right on the highway near Mabel's store. Then my mother was raised by her grandparents, but I never knew them either. They moved down to Florida when my mother married Zeke and they died down in Florida—I don't know what of—but they never came back here even for a visit. My mother had a fight with them or something."

"Maybe they didn't want her to marry Zeke."

"I don't see how that could be. Everybody likes Zeke. He's so good. He worked at the garage where my mother's grandparents got their car serviced, but the garage went out of business; so Zeke had to work at a meat-packing place in Rutland. He didn't like that job much."

"It must be hard for you to have your father on the road all the time."

"Yes, I miss him a lot."

"I bet your mother does too."

"Yes, she misses him."

"She's very young to have so many children."

"Oh, she's not as young as she looks. She's thirty-one," Shari said.

Mrs. Wallace laughed and said, "That's very young, Shari. Mabel says your mother had you and then your two older brothers all before she was twenty."

"I know," Shari said quickly. "But why'd she have us if she didn't want us?" She blushed, embarrassed at what she'd blurted out.

"Lots of women seem pretty vague about reproduction. They just get pregnant without thinking much about it. Anyway, if she doesn't have any more children, she could go out and get herself a job and that might make her happier."

"She won't have any more children," Shari said, remembering the weeks of nagging Charlotte had gone through to talk Zeke into having a vasectomy after Peter was born. "But I don't think she'll ever get a job."

"Why not?"

"She keeps making excuses."

"People do change, Shari."

"I suppose so." She couldn't imagine Charlotte changing. "What time is it, Mrs. Wallace?"

When Shari discovered that three hours had passed since she'd left home, she was dismayed. "I'd better go now," she said. "Peter must be wondering where I am."

"You don't mind being in charge of him so much at all, do you?" Mrs. Wallace asked.

"Mind? Oh, no. Peter and I are a pair."

Mrs. Wallace nodded as if she understood. It gave Shari pleasure to be so quickly understood.

She was on her way and almost out of earshot when Mrs. Wallace called, "Shari! I completely forgot to show you all that material on bird banding I got in the mail."

"I'll come back soon," Shari answered. "Maybe tomorrow."

Even before she had swung over the protruding lip above the ravine, she wished she hadn't said it. Being too sure of anything was risky. Expecting good luck sometimes brought on bad. She should have known from past experience never to take anything for granted, she thought despairingly at the sight of the red tee shirt in the bottom of the ravine.

She slipped and skidded down the steep graveled side and bent over Peter's still body. He was lying face down where he'd fallen, close to the stream.

"Petey?" He didn't move. "Petey?" She touched him. His body was warm, but his stillness terrified her. "Petey?" His eyes were closed and his face was smeared with blood and dirt. She remembered learning that you weren't supposed to move people if they had had a bad fall. Carefully she put her ear to his chest and held her breath. When she heard his heart beat, she left him lying there and raced across the log and up the ravine, running for home and help as fast as her fear could propel her.

Seven

Charlotte's wail made the disaster real to Shari.

"Peter's lying hurt in the bottom of the ravine," Shari had announced. Now she had to force herself past her screaming mother to the telephone, where Zeke had pasted emergency numbers for fire and police and the rescue squad. Tension made Shari's fingers so stiff that she had difficulty dialing, but finally the call went through. "My brother needs help," she said and briefly described where Peter had fallen. Charlotte yanked the phone from her hands to add a garbled plea for them to hurry.

Shari started back out to her brother, but Charlotte stopped her. "Don't you dare leave this house. You stay here and wait for Doug and Walter. I'll take care of Peter."

"But you don't know where he is and I do."

"I told you. Stay here," Charlotte said. Each word burned with hate as she added, "Do like I say for once. I'm going to my son now and I'll deal with you later."

Shari heard her mother starting her car. If Charlotte waited for the rescue squad at the bridge that crossed high over the ravine and directed them from there, they would enter the ravine too far from Peter. With no path to follow and rocks and brambles to hold them back, they'd take forever to get to him. Suppose Peter opened his eyes and found himself alone! Shari couldn't obey. She couldn't remain in the house doing nothing when Peter might need her.

She began running back along the shortcut. He was still unconscious when she reached him. She couldn't tell by listening for a heartbeat if he was alive or not because her breath was coming in gasps and her own heart pounded too loudly in her ears. Blood oozed from his hair. When she put her arms around him, he felt suspiciously cool. She kissed him and spoke to him and tried warming him with her body. Once she thought she saw his eyelids flutter, but she couldn't be sure.

"Petey, wake up. Petey, I love you so much. Please be all right," she begged. Sitting there on the damp ground, she shivered. How much colder he must feel! She wanted to get his body off the ground and onto her lap, but she was afraid to risk moving him. All she could do was wait. She didn't cry. She was too full of dread to cry.

She listened in the dark at the bottom of the ravine while the water warbled its way over the rocks and birds whistled to each other across the stream until, at last, she heard the voices of the rescue squad. "You see him anywheres?" "Not yet." "Think we're in the right place?"

"Here!" Shari yelled. "He's here, here, here." Her voice echoed. She kept screaming until she was hoarse and an answer came back.

"Okay, we hear you."

A lanky, gray-haired man and a chunky young woman in jeans came crashing through the thicket on the far bank. "There's a log you can cross the stream on," Shari yelled.

She heard them curse and encourage each other as they eased their way across. Then they were there to take charge. She felt hopeful now. They would take care of Peter.

"Is there a better way out than how we came in?" the woman asked Shari as the man wrapped Peter in a blanket and secured him to a stretcher.

"Kid's in shock," the man said softly.

"I'll show you the way. Follow me," Shari said and took off.

"Would've been easier if we'd known this route in the first place," the man said when she'd led them out. "You're some climber, honey, a first-class mountain goat."

Mourning doves cried sadly in the trees as they emerged into the late-afternoon sunlight. The man used his walkie-talkie to call the ambulance to meet them at the house. Charlotte drove up behind the ambulance and got in as they bundled Peter inside. They raced off with siren screaming.

Walter and Doug got home anxious to know what

had happened. They'd been told by neighbors that their brother had been killed.

"He's in shock," Shari said. "He'll be all right." She didn't know what shock was, except it was something that people lived through, came out of, something that passed.

"Where's Ma?" Doug asked.

"She went in the ambulance with Pete."

"You going to make supper?" Walter asked.

"No," Shari said. "You can make yourselves sandwiches if you're hungry." She was tired. Even her bones were tired, and her head hurt as if in sympathy with Peter's. The unfamiliar urge to cry overtook her.

She dragged up to her room and got an enthusiastic greeting from Blue Boy, who gripped the bars of his cage and bobbed his head and chattered as if he were questioning her. Wasn't she going to talk to him? Where had she been, leaving him alone so long? She looked at him helplessly and threw herself on her bed, choking on unshed tears.

Hours later she was sitting by the window in the dark listening to the intricate details of night business outside when a car stopped in front of the house and Charlotte's voice came clearly thanking someone for the ride. The door to the house closed. Shari stiffened. She thought of getting into bed and pretending to be asleep, but knew better than to hope she could escape her mother's wrath that way. She waited for the sound of Charlotte's footsteps on the stairs and held her breath as her mother stopped outside her door. One frightened part of Shari wanted to hide, and another part held fast to her old protective shield. Nothing can hurt me, that part of her said. No matter what she does, she can't touch me inside. Only this time, Peter was involved and that made Shari vulnerable. He had lain there so still with the blood on his face and in his hair. Waves of panic hit her just thinking of how still he had lain.

The door opened. Shari glanced at her mother's face, but she couldn't read it. Charlotte's expression was set in hard, tired lines with none of the prettiness that she showed Zeke.

"Aren't you going to ask about your brother?" Charlotte said. "Don't you want to know how he is?"

"Is he all right?"

"How could he be after what you did to him?"

"I didn't do anything."

"You took him down there to play, didn't you?"

"No, not today. He came by himself. I went to Mrs. Wallace's, and he didn't want to come with me, so I left him home. Then he must have changed his mind or something."

"You left him home?"

"You were here."

"I should have known better than to trust you with him. You've always been a rotten mean kid since the day you were born. Never a smile out of you. Never a hug or a kiss. Soon as you could walk, you ran away from me, never to me, always away. I thought you had feelings for him at least, but you let him fall down that ravine, and if he dies, you just better believe it was you killed him." She turned around and left, shutting first Shari's door and then her own behind her.

Shari crept to her bed and pulled the covers over her head. Inside her, everything was shattered ice. She couldn't get warm. One hope only stood out in the white glare of her mother's hatred. He wasn't dead yet. He hadn't died. And tomorrow, no matter what, Shari would go to the hospital and see him.

In the morning, Shari took care of Blue Boy first. As she cleaned out his cage, he sat on her shoulder, puffed out his throat feathers and ducked his head, chirring and squawking at her. She set out a dish of water for his bath in the bottom of his clean cage. He balanced in the doorway, which she'd fixed open by attaching it to the cage with a paper clip.

While he considered whether to bathe or not, she went about getting herself dressed for the visit to the hospital. She had to look old enough so they'd let her in. She didn't own a skirt, but she had a blouse with small pink rosebuds and a little round collar that would do, and she tied her hair back with a pink ribbon from a birthday package. Her sneakers were dirty, but she didn't have time to wash them.

Money. After someone had raided the glass jar in which she collected her money, she had begun to hide the occasional allowance Zeke gave her, and now she had to think a minute to recall where the last hiding place had been. In an envelope stuck to the back of her dresser drawer, she remembered, and eased the drawer out as quietly as she could. The envelope was there but it held only two dollars. She couldn't buy transportation with that, but she could get Petey some candy or cookies when she got to town. First, before she risked hitching, she'd see if Mabel had any deliveries going from the store in the right direction.

The house was quiet when Shari slipped out of her room. Her family was still sleeping. Her stomach reminded her that she hadn't eaten last night. In fact, she couldn't recall whether she'd had lunch yesterday or not. She'd better stop to eat something before she left, maybe take a sandwich with her in case she was gone all day.

She left a note on the kitchen table: "Went to see Peter." She didn't sign it, "Love." There was no love, had never been any according to what Charlotte said last night. From the moment of her birth, her mother had hated her. She wondered if she was feelingless as Charlotte claimed. The truth was, nobody mattered to her besides Peter now, and what she felt for him was cold fear, nothing as warm and caressing as love. Even Zeke seemed beyond range of her feelings. Except Shari wished he were here. He wouldn't blame her for Peter's fall, and Charlotte would be less dangerous if Zeke were home.

In her hurry, Shari dropped the peanut-butter jar. It didn't break, but rolled noisily on the vinyl floor, and when she finished making her sandwich and was ready to go, a voice said, "You little sneak. Where do you think you're going all dressed up?"

"To the hospital. I left you a note," Shari said quickly.

Charlotte stood there puffy faced in her transparent lavender nightgown. "You're not going nowhere," she said. "After what you did to him, you're not going near him. I told them not to let you into the hospital."

Shari knew it was a lie as soon as the words left her mother's mouth. "I'll tell Zeke if you don't let me go," Shari blurted out.

"You'll do what?" Charlotte took a step toward her,

eyes fierce. "What did you say to me? You'll do what?" She took another menacing step toward Shari.

"I know you don't love me," Shari said. "But Zeke does. He'll understand about Peter." She gasped and her hand went automatically to her head where her mother had knocked it against the corner of the kitchen cabinet. Blood oozed through her hair as her mother slapped her cheek, so hard that Shari fell down. Charlotte grabbed her and jerked her up, gripping her arms so that Shari couldn't protect her face, but Charlotte didn't want to hit her again.

"You think Zeke loves you?" Charlotte hissed into Shari's face. "You know how funny that is? Why would he love you when you're not even his own kid? How do you think you got to be such a narrow, skinny little rat? It's because you look like your father, that's how come. Just because Zeke lets you use his name don't mean he's your father. Your father ran away as soon as he found out I was pregnant. Not that I lost anything when I lost him. He wasn't much, let me tell you, about as loving as a rat, and you were born just like him." She shoved Shari away from her. "Now you go upstairs to your room and you stay there until I say you can come out, and don't you ever threaten to tell Zeke on me again. Don't you ever dare."

Charlotte stood watching as Shari fumbled her way to the stairs, swaying a little, having to lean against the wall as she climbed to keep her balance. Shari crept into her room. Blue Boy was vigorously flicking water drops from his bath in all directions. He fussed with his feathers, stretched out a wing, groomed it with his beak and then did the other. She watched him for a minute, but then she had to lie down on her bed. Her hair felt sticky from the blood oozing from the bump, which was swelling. Her cheek stung where Charlotte had slapped her, but the physical pain was outside her. Deep inside was the raw, burning hole Charlotte's direct hit had torn. The father whose love had given Shari all the comfort and reassurance there had been in life was gone, cut off from her as surely as if he were dead. Suddenly, Shari saw herself alone, not by her own choice, but by the chance of birth that had brought her to a mother who hated her and no father at all. A suffocating loneliness overcame her, shutting out thought, making it hard for her to breathe.

When her mind began to function again, it was only to deal with the immediate, the problem of how she would get to Peter. Patiently, she tried to reason it out, but each thought slipped away as she reached for it. Walter and Doug were stirring, getting up, going downstairs. Blue Boy rested on his swing looking content with himself as the bright morning sun lit up his cage. The patch of sky in the top corner of her window promised a perfect summer day. Still Shari lay on her bed, too groggy to move.

Someone knocked at her door. "Who is it?" she asked.

The door opened and Walter stuck his head in. "She's gone to the hospital," he said. "She said she'll be gone all day. You want anything?"

"No, thank you."

He waited, then he said, "Well, if you want anything, I'll get it for you before Doug and me go to his stand. . . . I could lend you a book."

"Did she tell you how Peter is?"

"He's got a concussion, she said. I don't know what that means."

"Me either." He kept standing there, so she smiled at him for his kindness, for stepping out of his normal indifference to try to help her.

Awkwardly, he shifted from one foot to the other. "Well, if you need anything . . ." he said and waited.

"Nothing, thanks." Finally he left.

The problem of how to get around Charlotte's presence in Peter's hospital room and find out if he was all right lay snarled in Shari's mind. At last she began to untangle it. Mabel—she always heard everything. Shari could get her to call and find out from Charlotte how Peter really was.

Shari got to her feet and down the stairs and out of the empty house. She walked down the road, so intent on getting to Mabel's store that she barely noticed her physical discomfort. The store was empty. Mabel was sitting on the porch reading a western from the paperback rack, her reading glasses halfway down her long nose, earrings dangling, long hair pulled back and curling on her forehead, and one long thin leg crossed over the other and swinging rhythmically.

"What's the matter, Shari honey? You look done in," Mabel said looking over the tops of her glasses.

"Have you heard about Peter?"

"I'll say I did. Poor little fella. I was here when the rescue wagon went roaring by. What happened to your face?"

"Nothing," Shari said. "Mabel, do you think you could call my mother and ask her how Peter is?"

"Call your mother? Where is she? Oh, sure, don't mind me. She must've went to the hospital."

"Yes," Shari said. "Could you call and ask about Peter? I mean, like it's *you* wants to know? Don't tell her it's me asking."

"Why not?" Mabel's homely face knotted in confusion.

"Because she's mad at me," Shari said and shrugged and tried to smile as her eyes fell away.

"You don't mean she blames you for what happened to Peter?"

Shari nodded.

"Well, that's nonsense. She'll get over that. Don't you worry, honey. You're the best big sister any boy could have. You just can't be holding on to him every single minute, that's all; and boys will get into trouble the minute you turn your back on them. Want me to tell her that?"

"No. Please, don't say anything about me at all. Please? Just call and ask how Peter is."

"Ummmm." Mabel reached out bony fingers to touch Shari's cheek. "That's some nasty bruise you've got. Looks like whoever you were fighting got you good. And what's that on your head?"

Shari drew back. "It's nothing. I'm all right. Please call, Mabel."

"Sure, I can do that easy enough. Come inside. Want a soda? It's on the house." Mabel went to the phone on the wall at the back of the store. While she was dialing, Shari stood before the glass-fronted cooler looking at the stacks of colorful soda cans and bottles inside. A wave of dizziness washed over her. The peanut-butter sandwich probably still lay on the kitchen floor where it had fallen when Charlotte grabbed her.

". . . Well, if there's no telephone in the room, could

you get Mrs. Lally to call Mabel at the store, please?" Mabel said into the phone. A few seconds later she hung up and said, "Come sit outside with me a minute, Shari. Your ma will likely call back."

Shari asked if she might take a pint container of milk instead of soda.

"Sure. You *are* looking peaked, child. Have one of these doughnuts too. I already opened the package to treat myself this morning. . . . Shari? Are you all right?"

When Shari came to, Mabel told her she had fainted. "Your mother called, and I told her how you was so worried you'd come down here and had me call to find out how your little brother was doing, and then you'd fainted right away. Scared me half to death passing out like that. . . . Here, sip some of this cold milk. Not too many sisters dote on their little brothers the way you do on Peter, I told her. I don't think she's mad at you anymore. She said— Are you feeling better now? Don't move; just sip the milk slow and easy. Shocks will do that to you—make the blood run clear out of your head. I fainted once myself—would you believe it, big as I am? Fainted in the doctor's office when they stitched up my little grandson. He didn't pass out; I did." She laughed at herself.

"What did she say about Peter?" Shari asked wearily. Mabel had done her in by letting Charlotte know that Shari'd left the house. Mabel had just gotten rattled and talked. She hadn't understood at all why Shari didn't want her to tell. Better not to think about the consequences she'd have to face when Charlotte got home.

"Peter's doing all right, just fine," Mabel said. "A little woozy from the concussion is all."

"But he's awake? He's not unconscious anymore?"

"Well, I don't know. Must be awake. Anyway, she said to tell you to go home and wait for her there. She'll be back by supper time."

"She's not bringing Peter home?"

"Not yet, honey. But don't you worry. He's got a head hard as a rock, that little fella. He'll be just fine. Looks like you got hit on the head yourself. Did you do that yesterday? When you was in the ravine?"

"I . . . don't know," Shari said.

Mabel sighed. "Sometimes," she said kindly, "when a parent gets riled, they strike out at whoever's around. My papa used to backhand us every once in a while, hit us so hard our ears would ring, and he'd keep on walking just like he'd never done a thing. It taught us to be careful how we acted around him, but he didn't mean us no harm. Just wanted to see we were brought up good and proper. Your mama's grandma—you know, the one who raised Charlotte—she had a heavy hand, believed a good spanking cured a lot of things."

"I'd better get back home," Shari said.

"How about I give you a lift?"

"No, thank you. I can walk."

"Nonsense," Mabel said. "I'll just shut the store for a few minutes and take you home." Without giving Shari a chance to argue, she flipped the sign on the door to CLOSED and shut the door behind them as she ushered Shari out to the car parked in front.

"You've got a nice family," Mabel said as she backed out of the driveway. "Doug and Walter are such good, hard-working boys, and Zeke is as steady a fella as anybody could want for a father, but your mama's a little on the nervous side, and she's alone with the four of you too much. You got to be a good child and help her and maybe not go running off in the woods all the time like she complains you do."

Shari heard Mabel's words, but they glanced off her as if Mabel were talking about some other family. The only one Shari still felt bound to was Peter. The others had been cut off from her. More than ever before in her life, she was outside, apart and alone.

Mabel stopped the car in Shari's driveway and looked at her. "You know, your mama was a real goody-goody little girl growing up," Mabel said and went rambling on. "Her grandmother was just as proud of how well behaved and neat and sweet she was. Of course, when Charlotte got to high school, she made up for it. Used to cut school and fool around where she oughtn't to of been. People used to say things that weren't so nice about her, and then she married Zeke before she even graduated. That shut the gossips up, because everybody liked Zeke, you know. Anyway, why I'm telling you this is, it's likely your mama's afraid you're getting too wild and that you'll suffer for it like she did."

Shari made a sound somewhere between a laugh and a cry. Mabel was so far off the mark that it was funny. "Thanks for the ride," Shari said and tried to get the door open.

Mabel reached over and opened it for her. "You feeling wobbly still?"

"I'm fine," Shari said automatically. She offered up as much of a smile as she could manage and got out of the car and around to the back door.

The peanut-butter sandwich she'd made was still on the floor. She picked it up and threw it in the garbage pail. She'd have to eat soon, even though she felt too nauseous now. She needed her strength if she was going to get herself out of the house before Charlotte got home tonight. She'd deliberately disobeyed her mother, not once, but several times. What would Charlotte do to her? A flash of memory brought back that hand with the long enameled fingernails as it lifted the screen up on Shari's window. She'd been in the tree outside, and her mother's hand at her screen had puzzled her until Shari saw Chirpy fly out. She'd scrambled from her tree and chased him into the woods, calling, but he wouldn't come back, and Charlotte would never admit it was her fault. Charlotte didn't even remember what she'd done. And Zeke loved Charlotte. Did he love Charlotte's child too, or had he just been kind all these years, pretending to be Shari's father? Unless Charlotte had kept her secret even from him.

Eight

Her heaviness as she climbed through the ravine did not come from the cage she carried with Blue Boy inside clinging to its bars by claws and beak and flapping his wings for balance. The heaviness wasn't even her worry about Peter, but something deeper. Shari concentrated on boxing it away in the furthest recesses of her mind where it couldn't hurt her. She did the trick that usually worked. She concentrated hard on some immediate task, in this case figuring out how to persuade Mrs. Wallace to keep Blue Boy for her. Even if that bird-loving lady were willing, she would want to know why Shari needed the favor. Shari poked around her mind for an excuse, but she still had no words ready when she knocked on Mrs. Wallace's door.

"Come in, Mabel," Mrs. Wallace called.

"No, it's me," Shari said and hesitated on the threshold. She saw Mrs. Wallace standing at the oven. A delicious smell of baking bread filled the airy kitchen. Breakfast dishes were draining in a wooden rack, and a ruby-red vase on the windowsill had caught a sunbeam.

"Shari! You came just in time. When I got the urge to bake this dill bread, I hoped somebody would come by and share it with me." Mrs. Wallace stood up and set the steaming loaf she was holding by two oven mitts on a hot pad on the table.

"Come sit down," Mrs. Wallace said. "Why do you have your bird with you?" And then, as she focused on Shari more closely, she asked, "What's wrong?" Her gray eyes narrowed with concern. "What happened to you?"

"Nothing," Shari said. "Would you be willing to take care of Blue Boy for me for a while?"

"Take care of him? Are you going somewhere?"

"Well . . . I don't know. But my little brother's in the hospital, and if . . . I just don't have time to take care of Blue Boy right now, and I thought—"

"Shari, who hit you?"

Shari shook her hair forward and bent her head to hide her face. "Nobody," she said. "It just happened. It isn't anything."

"Isn't it?" Mrs. Wallace lifted Shari's chin and studied her cheek, then gently probed the lump on Shari's head. "This needs to be seen to. Sit here, and while we're waiting for the bread to cool, I'll practice my first aid on you." Her calmness put Shari at ease.

"I took a course," Mrs. Wallace continued. "Figured living up on the mountain by myself, I should know a thing or two about cuts and bruises." She kept talking from the other room and returned quickly with a first-aid box and towels. Shari let her work on the tender place on her head.

"Am I hurting you?" Mrs. Wallace asked as she washed away the dried blood from around the lump with warm, soapy water.

"No," Shari said.

"You're a stoic."

"What's that?"

"It's a person who stands up to pain well and doesn't mind hardship. Comes from people who lived in ancient Greece. They were known for being able to take hard knocks without complaining. . . . Why did your mother hit you?"

"She didn't."

"I heard about what happened to your little brother. Mabel called me this morning. Did he fall while you were with me yesterday?"

"Yes. He must have changed his mind and come after me, but he couldn't make it over the ledge alone, so he fell," Shari said. She heard her voice go high on the last words.

"Well, you couldn't help that."

"I'm supposed to watch out for him."

"Every minute of the day?"

Shari hunched her shoulders.

"Your mother is responsible for Peter except when you're with him alone."

To her own astonishment, Shari burst out, "But she hates me. She says it's my fault. And now she won't even let me go see him. Mabel says he's all right, but he looked like he was dead when I found him yesterday."

"And you ran home and told your mother, and she

blamed you. Is that it?" Mrs. Wallace didn't wait for an answer. She insisted, "You can't help what your brother does when you're not with him."

"I told him he could do it. I said he was as good a climber as me, but he's not, and he fell." Shari shuddered. Now her head ached horribly.

"What I don't understand," Mrs. Wallace said, "is what all this has to do with your parakeet."

"Because my mother's mad at me."

Mrs. Wallace whistled softly. "I see," she said. They both heard a car crunching on the gravel driveway. "I invited Mabel up for lunch today. You stay too, Shari. I've got homemade blackberry preserves and some good cheese and tomatoes to go with the dill bread."

"Thank you, but—" Shari began her exercise in polite refusal, but Mrs. Wallace interrupted her.

"Stay. I'll take care of Blue Boy as long as you need, but I'll expect you to come visit him often. All right?"

"Yes, thank you," Shari said. She felt so weak, and it felt good just to sit there in the pleasant kitchen and be cared for and fed.

"Well, look who's here!" Mabel said.

"Take a load off your feet, Mabel," Mrs. Wallace said. "Shari's joining our lunch party today."

"Now, isn't that nifty. I see you've been doctoring her some."

"I'm thinking of paying a visit to Shari's mother tomorrow," Mrs. Wallace announced.

"Don't do that," Mabel said. "Hereabouts that'd be considered nosing around in other people's business."

"Some things require interference."

"Nosy neighbors are not appreciated in this part of the country, Eve. I'm warning you."

"All I'm going to do is pay a social call on Shari's mother."

"You've lived up here—how many years—and you've never seen fit to call on Charlotte Lally before. What are you going to say that you come about?"

"Shari wants me to take care of her bird for her. I'll get her mother's permission. How's that, Mabel? Also I can inquire after my friend, Peter."

"Makes no difference to me, as long as you don't go busting in there telling her how to bring up her children. You know, lots of folks don't see nothing wrong in a smack to keep a kid from getting out of hand. Don't you go making a federal case out of nothing."

"What makes you think I'd do that?"

"That look in your eye," Mabel said. "I've known you long enough to recognize when you got your back up."

"Tell me, Mabel, if you saw a parent beating up her child in front of your store, would you sit and watch or jump up and try to stop her?"

"Shari's parents don't beat her up." Mabel sounded horrified. She turned toward Shari. "Do they?"

"No," Shari said, denying what she had always denied even to herself.

"Then what's that hand-shaped bruise on her cheek and the bump on her head from?" Mrs. Wallace asked.

"Shari?" Mabel demanded support in setting Mrs. Wallace straight.

"It's nothing," Shari said. She was protecting not just Charlotte from shame, but her brothers and father and herself as well. Deep down inside her was the guilty sense that she had to be the cause of the wrong that was done her.

"There, you see?" Mabel said to Mrs. Wallace. "This

child comes from a perfectly good family. I've known her mother all her life. She's not a bad woman. Maybe Charlotte's grandparents was stricter than they should've been and kept her to home and protected her overmuch. Then she got herself a husband who did the same, until he decided to go off on the road and leave her in charge of four growing kids, which is more than her nerves can stand—"

"Then good neighbors should offer to relieve her when it becomes too much for her nerves," Mrs. Wallace said briskly.

"So long as you don't come right out and accuse Charlotte of nothing," Mabel said. "It wouldn't do Shari no good either, you know. Where's she going to go that's better than her own home?"

"Here if she likes."

Mabel was silenced by the answer. Shari looked at Mrs. Wallace in a daze. "I could come here to stay?" she asked.

"Why not?" Mrs. Wallace said firmly. "I have those two empty beds up in the attic that my granddaughters seldom use. Plenty of space and time." She smiled. "That would be one way to ensure your help in the bird-banding project, Shari."

"Oh, Mrs. Wallace!"

"There," Mrs. Wallace said comfortingly as Shari hid her face in her hands. "There, there. It's just an offer, something you can think about anyway. Meanwhile, let's eat lunch."

Shari went to the bathroom to recover her composure. When she'd washed her hands and returned, Mrs. Wallace and Mabel were talking about the problem of setting up the large nylon-mesh nets to catch the migratory birds without hurting them so they could be banded and set free.

"They're just like square sails, I believe, and the birds fly into them and tangle their feet and make a pouch in the mesh. Then you've got to go around several times a day to free them. 'Course clipping the little metal band on only takes a few seconds, and after you release them, you make a record of it. I've seen it done, but I've never tried it myself," Mrs. Wallace was saying.

Shari ate some of the crusty, tender dill bread. It tasted better than anything she could remember. She had a second slice and then a third. The warmth in the kitchen from the oven and the fuzziness in her head began to make her very sleepy.

"You lie down and take a nap on my bed," the observant Mrs. Wallace said. She guided Shari into a room with lilac-colored walls and a lilac print bedspread. Beside the bed were shelves of interesting objects—a painted lace-edged fan, a china ballerina, shells bigger than the biggest pinecones, a fat, funny bowling-pin-shaped doll, a silver coach. The crystal bird was there too.

"May I hold it?" Shari pointed, as Mrs. Wallace threw a rose-and-gray knitted afghan over her.

"Of course." Mrs. Wallace put the bird in her hands. "It's yours for as long as you need it." She left the room.

Shari closed her eyes gratefully. Before she awoke, she dreamed that she was standing at the end of Peter's hospital bed looking over a rolling bed tray at her little brother's pale, round face.

"Are you really all right?" she asked him.

"Shari? Where were you? I missed you."

"I'm here now. You know I'd be with you if I could, Petey Pie."

"Hug me, Shari," Peter said, and she did, reassured by the solid feel of him in her arms that he was going to be well soon.

She came out of Mrs. Wallace's bedroom feeling renewed. Mabel was just leaving and offered Shari a lift home.

"Yes, thank you," Shari said. Then she hesitated. She wanted to let Mrs. Wallace know how grateful she was for all the kindnesses of the afternoon, and most of all for the promise of a refuge. Just saying thank you wasn't enough. So Shari did the only thing that came to her. She put her arms shyly around Mrs. Wallace's stocky form and hugged her.

"There, there," Mrs. Wallace said, looking pleased and patting Shari's back. "If you need me, just call."

"Did you really mean that I could take the crystal bird with me?" Shari asked.

"That's what I mean," Mrs. Wallace said. "And I mean what I said about living here too." She wrapped the bird in a paper towel, and Shari carried it off in her hand. It was precious now, not only because of its beauty, but because it was proof of Mrs. Wallace's belief in her.

Nine

Charlotte was in a good mood at supper that night. As she served them a salad of cold tuna fish and mixed vegetables with mayonnaise, she told them, "The doctor says Peter could've been crippled or brain damaged from that fall, but likely he won't be. No thanks to you, Miss Shari Ape Face. Where'd you spend the day? Out in the woods again?"

"I took Blue Boy over to Mrs. Wallace's and left him there."

"What for?" The sharp edge of Charlotte's voice jabbed Doug into attention, and even Walter looked up from the book he was reading at the table.

"I don't feel like taking care of Blue Boy right now, not until Pete is well," Shari said and added, "Mrs.

Wallace may come by to see you. She wants to ask if it's all right if she keeps my bird."

"You crazy? What do I care what she does with it? Make her pay for the cage though if she ends up keeping him for good." Charlotte looked at her suspiciously. "Did you tell her anything?"

"About what?"

"About how much you hate your mother, or anything like that."

"I don't tell things," Shari said. "Anyway, you're the one hates me." As soon as the words left her mouth, Shari stood up and backed away from the table, afraid that she'd triggered an explosion.

"Sit down," Charlotte said. "I'm not going to hit you. I only got mad at you because you let Peter hurt himself. Don't start pretending to be scared of me all of a sudden. You've never been scared of me in your life."

"I don't like getting hit," Shari said.

"I don't hit you. A slap once in a while isn't hitting. And *you* don't feel it anyway. Don't feel nothing, never did. Even when you were tiny, you didn't cry. I used to wonder if you were human, the way nothing seemed to hurt you."

"She cries," Walter said quickly. "I've seen her."

"You have?" Charlotte glanced at him and away. "Well, you've seen more than me then," she said bitterly and began to clear away the dishes.

Shari hadn't finished eating, but she took her plate to the sink anyway.

"I got invited to go fishing tomorrow," Doug said. "You want to take my place at the stand with Walter, Shari?"

"Okay," she agreed, pleased he would trust her.

"We'll pay you a percentage of whatever we make. Not a lot. Say ten percent, maybe twenty depending on how good a day it is."

"That's okay." Shari would have offered to do it for nothing, but she thought she could use the money to bring Peter something nice. "Whatever you want to give me would be fine."

Alone in her room, she stood idly thinking that tomorrow would be a pleasant day in the shade of the tree where the boys had set up their vegetable stand. Walter would read in between customers while she watched the cars go by and made change and bagged the corn and tomatoes people bought. Hours would pass quickly, bringing her another day closer to when Peter would come home and another day closer to when Zeke would return. She had something to ask Zeke, and if his answer told her that she had been mistaking kindness for love, then her whole life was going to change.

She knelt on her bed at the window listening to the lulling night sounds—the cry of a hunting bird, the peep and buzz of insects, the swish of passing cars—all interwoven with the whisper of the wind through the leaves. But the web of sound failed to soothe her as it usually did. An ache was swelling in her chest, expanding so fast she was afraid she couldn't contain it. It came from the words Charlotte had spoken. It dealt with who Shari was, and she feared that if she recognized it, she would become another person, someone without anyone at all to love.

Walter and Shari straggled in from their day at the

vegetable stand to find Charlotte lying on a folding metal lounge chair in the driveway, smoking and reading one of the movie magazines she regularly borrowed from BeeJay's shop.

"Your friend stopped by," Charlotte said to Shari. "She seems quite taken with you. Brought me some kind of bread she made. She said you and her have a lot in common, the way you like birds and all. I told her it was all right with me if she wants to keep your parakeet at her place."

"Good," Shari said, relieved that Mrs. Wallace's visit hadn't made Charlotte angry.

"She invited me to come by her house," Charlotte continued. "I told her that dirt road of hers was too much for me to drive with my old junker. I don't have no four-wheel-drive pickup like she's got. . . . Guess she likes being alone up there."

"She doesn't mind being alone," Shari agreed.

"Like you. Looks like you're a pair, you and that weird old lady."

"She's not weird," Shari said.

"Well, just don't hang around her too much or you'll wear out your welcome."

"I won't wear it out." A breathlessness overtook Shari, and then she lashed out at Charlotte with a boast. "Mrs. Wallace said I could come and live with her if I want."

"She said that in so many words?"

"Yes."

"And you'd go?"

"I might."

"Just what I'd expect from you. Pick up and leave us just like that!" Charlotte illustrated with a snap of her fingers. "Like your own family don't mean a thing to you."

"Shari," Walter said, "aren't you going to wait till Pete gets out of the hospital?"

"I don't know," Shari said feeling powerful.

Charlotte's eyes were filled with tears as she teetered between being hurt and being furious. The fury won. "Don't you dare go to that woman. We're your family here. We're your family and you belong with us."

"But I don't," Shari said. "You told me yourself I don't belong to anybody here except you, and *you* hate me." She was flying, flying over the abyss, amazed at her own recklessness.

"Run, Shari," Walter yelled. He left the carport and the unsold food they'd brought back and stepped toward her, then stopped. She saw Charlotte rising from her lounge chair, saw her lunge, hand raised to strike.

Instinctively, Shari dashed toward the woods. She thought of heading for Mrs. Wallace's house, but realized that was the first place Charlotte would check. Up the mountain then. Shari zigzagged through the trees toward Eagle's Perch. Why had she let the words fly out of her like that? She'd been guarding her tongue all her life, but lately it seemed whenever she opened her mouth, words flew out—to Mrs. Wallace, to Charlotte, whose anger was so easily roused. Shari couldn't understand what had gotten into her. Her ability to control herself had always been her greatest protection.

On the ledge near the narrow peak of the mountain, hours later, she watched the shadows sweep across the valley floor. The pale evening sky turned up a single star. The darkness rose up from the earth and spread heavenward. As the knowledge she had tried to hide from crept up on her, she wished she had some charm to give her courage. Even the crystal bird would have helped. But it was in her room, hidden in her boot. Zeke was not her father. But what was even worse— Peter was not really her brother. Her only real relative was Charlotte. Shari mourned the family she had lost. Hour after hour, she mourned, hour after hour until the pain burned itself out and even the ashes were cooling.

At last she began to feel her way back down in the moonlight to the only place she could go to escape her mother's wrath. She walked in open spaces now because it was too dark to see beneath the trees. By midnight, she was knocking on Mrs. Wallace's door.

Mrs. Wallace opened the door, wearing a nightgown under a plaid flannel robe. Her face was as fresh and firm and her white hair as neat as during the day. "What are you doing roaming around in the middle of the night, Shari?" she asked.

"I saw your light. I thought you might be awake."

"So I am. Come on in. I've been reading a dull book about railroads. Dull books either put me to sleep or teach me enough to make being awake worthwhile. Try it sometime if you have trouble sleeping."

Without asking Shari whether she was hungry or not, Mrs. Wallace sat her down at the kitchen table and started putting food in front of her. "Pick at that chicken while I heat up this milk for hot chocolate. Or would you prefer it cold?"

"However you like it," Shari said.

"Hot then. . . . The police came by this evening."

Mrs. Wallace glanced at Shari as she spoke. "Seems your mother sent them. I expect we'd better call and tell her you're all right."

"You said yesterday I could live with you. Did you mean it?" Shari asked.

"Yes. You realize it will only work if your folks agree to allow it. Otherwise we'd have to go to court, and that could be a long and messy business."

Instead of considering that problem, Shari thought of Peter. He'd come home from the hospital and he'd miss her if she wasn't there. Even if he wasn't her real brother, he would miss her. Of course, she could spend time with him still—unless Charlotte wouldn't let him see her anymore. "My mother got angry when I told her you said I could live with you."

"I know," Mrs. Wallace said dryly. "She gave me what for over the phone for trying to steal your affections."

"I don't know why she cares, because she doesn't care about me," Shari said.

"Do you want to wait until your father comes home and talk it over with him?" Mrs. Wallace asked.

"I don't have a father," Shari said.

Mrs. Wallace poured Shari's hot chocolate into a mug and brought it to her, then filled a mug for herself. Finally, she sat down and said, "That's some statement." A moth flew crazily at the light of the umbrella-shaped lamp hanging over them. "Did your mother tell you that—that you don't have a father?"

"Yes."

"And that's why you ran away tonight?"

"Not exactly. Except, I guess what happened tonight was because it made me so mad that— I don't know.

It's awful to find out you're not who you thought. All my life I thought Zeke was my father."

"And you were glad of that?"

"Oh, yes. Zeke's wonderful. He's good to me. Only, he loves my mother best, of course."

"You're hurting, Shari. I can see it."

"Yes, I hurt," Shari admitted, "worse than anything."

"Did Charlotte tell you who your natural father is?"

"No. I didn't think to ask. She didn't like him much—after. She said he left her when—" Shari's voice trailed off, silenced by the old habit of not telling private family business.

"Maybe your mother didn't like him just because he left her. It's possible you might have a perfectly nice father somewhere, Shari."

Shari shook her head. "I don't care. Even if Zeke isn't my father, I don't need anybody else beside him."

"I'd tell him that if I were you."

"Tell him?"

"That you love him. Sure. Chances are he loves you as much as you do him."

"Do you think he knows he's not my real father?"

"What do you think?"

Shari considered. "I could ask him when he comes back. Then—if you wouldn't mind, I'll come and live with you, Mrs. Wallace."

"Mind?" Mrs. Wallace said. "It would be a treat for me. You're close to the age of my grandchildren, just between the youngest and the oldest. It would be like having a third granddaughter around."

The statement touched Shari, and she didn't know what to say, but Mrs. Wallace understood without words. She patted Shari's hand. "Why don't you go visit with Blue Boy while I call your mother to tell her you're safe."

"I'd rather you called the police and let them tell her," Shari said.

"Just as you please," Mrs. Wallace said.

When Mrs. Wallace reached the sheriff's office, she was told to keep Shari where she was. The sheriff would come for her. Mrs. Wallace hung up and said, "I guess you have to go home tonight whether I want you to or not."

Shari looked unhappy.

"You know," Mrs. Wallace said, "my good friend Mabel believes that every mother loves her child and that it's a child's duty to love her back. Do you think Mabel's right?"

"I don't know." It was the kind of subject Shari avoided thinking about. She looked at Mrs. Wallace, who was patiently waiting for an answer. For her sake, Shari tried. "Sometimes you just can't love somebody. And I guess some children aren't very lovable. I guess . . . I don't know."

"Well, I do," Mrs. Wallace said. "I've seen mothers who don't love their children and some who seem to pick on one particular child in a mean way. It can also happen that a mother doesn't have much love in her to give. And sometimes a mother and child don't fit well together and get on each other's nerves. It's not that the child is bad, or even that the mother is, it's just that they can't get along well living together. It's remarkable how little most families are like our ideal of how they should be."

"I hate my mother," Shari said in a husky voice. "Sometimes I really hate her." She held her breath in surprise at what she had said. She had never let the thought surface before, never opened that particular box. The closest she had ever come was thinking that Charlotte was the one doing the hating.

If Mrs. Wallace was shocked, she didn't show it. All she said was, "When you're older and on your own, you may understand your mother better and forgive her."

"I won't forgive her," Shari said. "She took Zeke and Peter away from me."

"Shari, she couldn't do that. She doesn't have the power. You'll see." Mrs. Wallace took her hand and squeezed it.

Shari didn't argue, but this time she knew Mrs. Wallace was wrong.

When the sheriff arrived, red-eyed and tired looking, Mrs. Wallace was showing Shari the guest beds up in the attic where her grandchildren usually slept. Mrs. Wallace offered the sheriff a cup of coffee, but he refused politely and said to Shari, "Let's get cracking, girl. Your poor mother's not going to sleep until she gets her baby girl home safe and sound."

"I hope her poor mother has her temper under control tonight," Mrs. Wallace said coolly and tipped Shari's chin up toward the light so that the sheriff could see her cheek. Shari had forgotten that Charlotte's hand was imprinted there in purple.

"I see," he said. "Well, if there's any trouble, I'll expect someone to report it."

"I'll report it if I hear about it," Mrs. Wallace said.

"You got any problem with going home now, young lady?" the sheriff asked, bending his wavy gray hair and veiny nose toward Shari so he could watch her expression as she answered him.

"I'll be okay," she said.

"She's a spunky girl," Mrs. Wallace informed the sheriff.

"All right, all right. I'll let the woman know her child's got friends. That's all it takes usually, just a hint or two."

"Tomorrow morning," Mrs. Wallace said to Shari, "I'll just stop by your house for a minute and see how you're doing. Okay?"

"Give Blue Boy a kiss for me when he wakes up," Shari told Mrs. Wallace.

Shari stepped out of the sheriff's car to find Charlotte waiting for her with open arms. It was the first hug her mother had given her in years.

"Guess everything is all right here for now. You call if you need me again," the sheriff said as he left. It wasn't clear whether he was talking to Shari or Charlotte.

"Zeke called in tonight, and I told him you were gone and to get home fast," Charlotte said breathlessly. "He's going to deliver the load he's got now and be back here by tomorrow night, but before that, you and me got some talking to do."

Alone in her room, Shari reached into her boot and withdrew the crystal bird. She could live so peacefully with Mrs. Wallace, but what if that meant living without Peter? It would become difficult to see him, and when she saw him, suppose they had become strangers to one another. Her longing to see him at that very moment was immense. She was so afraid of losing him again. The first time had been in the ravine when she thought that he was dead. This time it would be by her own choice. It was clear to her that she needed Peter more than he needed her. He had a family, but she was only his half sister and Doug and Walter's half sister and no blood relation to Zeke at all. She had nobody. Her whole life she had believed herself to be part of a family and half of a loving pair, but all she had now was Charlotte. She grasped the crystal bird tightly, trying to squeeze comfort from its smooth weight, but nothing eased the agony, not even the tears that finally came.

Charlotte's touch on her shoulder made Shari open her eyes. "You overslept. It's nearly noon. You never slept this late before. Tired yourself out with all your running yesterday, didn't you?"

Cautiously, Shari looked at her mother. Charlotte was bright faced and eager looking, girlish in jeans and tight green tee shirt that matched her eyes.

"Zeke's coming," Shari said, remembering.

"Should be here by supper time. Thanks to you and your shenanigans. What'd you run away for like that?"

Shari could detect no anger in her mother's voice. Probably Charlotte was glad of an excuse to get Zeke back early.

"Was it true what you told me, that he's not my father?" Shari dared to ask, at the same time automatically drawing back to the far corner of her bed and pulling her knees protectively against her chest.

"You want to hear about it?" Charlotte sounded curiously friendly. Without waiting for Shari's answer, she settled onto the bed and drew her knees up, clasping her hands around them in a mirror image of Shari's posture. "I was just a high-school kid," Charlotte began. "I was pretty and all the boys were after me, but your father was the one I wanted. Don't ask me why. He never had much to say for himself, and he was only a wiry little dark fellow, no handsome football type, let me tell you. He gave flying lessons at the airport, and he was a lot older than me, but I went with him. . . . He left me when I told him I was pregnant. Picked up and ran off even though he was twenty-five and I was only a kid. He didn't love me at all like he said." Her voice tightened. "What he loved was flying. Later on, I heard on the news that he got killed skydiving. I used to have dreams watching him fall through the sky. Not that it bothered me. He didn't care about me. Why should I feel bad about him? Anyways, instead of going into fashion like I'd wanted, I married Zeke and had you and that's what I got your father to thank for."

"So he's dead."

"Yes, but don't waste time grieving about that. He wasn't much, believe me."

"Did you love Zeke?"

"When I married him? Not then. He was just an older guy who'd always been sweet on me. I used to get him to drive me out to the airport sometimes, and he'd give me a hard time about cutting school. Not that the school ever knew. They had my program so messed up that I could leave after homeroom, and my teachers never did figure out where I was supposed to be. If my grandparents had known, they'd of killed me."

Shari didn't stir, and Charlotte went on talking. "They wanted to kill poor Zeke when we eloped because they thought he was the one. If he'd of given me the money to have an abortion like I wanted instead of marrying me, it would've worked out better." Charlotte's face creased with pain. "My grandparents were so mad at me! They packed up and moved to Florida and didn't write or call until after Walter was born. Then they wanted me to come down for a visit, but how could I with three little kids? And it got them that I never finished high school. I never did get up the courage to tell them it wasn't Zeke's fault I got pregnant. Nobody knew that, just Zeke and me."

"Were your grandparents nice?" Shari asked, feeling a sympathy for her mother that she'd never experienced before.

"Well, they weren't easy." Charlotte's voice sharpened. "They wouldn't have suited *you,* the way you like to run around as you please. They raised me good and proper."

"And you loved them?"

"Sure I did. . . . Well, anyways, they left me their money when they died, and that's how we come to buy this house. It was their money we used. Of course, I wanted to buy a place in the city instead, but Zeke wouldn't move away from here." A long sigh escaped her.

"I told you Mrs. Wallace says I can live with her," Shari said.

"So?"

"So I might go."

"You *would* want to do something like that. You would go and disgrace us by moving in with a stranger like we don't provide for you good."

"I'm not trying to disgrace you. It's just—"

"Oh, don't do me any favors. My friends'll know the truth. I try hard to be a good mother even though I get sick to death of it. Nobody sees *me* running around the bars at night like some women whose husbands are gone all the time. *You're* the one's going to look bad if you move out of here, not me."

"I don't care what people think," Shari said quietly.

"No, that's one of your big problems. You don't care about anyone but yourself."

"That's not true," Shari said as Charlotte rose and started out of the room.

"Who do you care about then?" Charlotte asked. Her face was flushed as she looked back over her shoulder at Shari.

"Peter and Zeke. And Mrs. Wallace."

"There's someone else should mean more to you," Charlotte said bitterly and jerked the door shut behind her.

The crystal bird dug into Shari's elbow when she sat up. She pressed its coolness to her cheek, then tucked the bird back into the boot and got dressed thinking about Charlotte's revelations. That her father had been a pilot struck Shari as a sign. He had given her something whether he had wanted to or not, his agility and his yearning to sail weightlessly across the sky. She had been born to be a flyer, and she would not let anyone stop her from becoming one. She would not be like her mother who'd been frustrated all her life in everything she'd wanted to do. Charlotte had never gotten what she wanted, not the husband nor the career, nor even the location to live. If only Charlotte were less spiteful, Shari could pity her. As it was, even understanding her mother's bitterness didn't help Shari to forgive her.

The sudden racket of an angry blue jay in the tree outside Shari's window reminded her of Blue Boy. Living with Mrs. Wallace meant having him back again, but what she still needed to figure out was how to hang on to Peter. If only she could take Peter along with her! Before she made Charlotte angry, she should have asked when Pete was coming home. Charlotte could so easily refuse to let Shari visit him, and he couldn't get through the ravine by himself. He couldn't go the long miles by the highway either, unless someone drove him. She had better talk to Zeke before she made any final decisions.

When Shari came out of the bathroom, she saw Charlotte getting car keys out of her shoulder bag and grabbing a pack of cigarettes from an open carton. "I'm going to the hospital," Charlotte said.

"How is Petey?"

"Okay. Coming along at least."

"Can I go with you?"

"No, you stay here. Peter might as well get used to not having you around since you're moving out on us." Charlotte tossed her head and left.

Shari had an urge to run after her and plead to go along, but she knew it was useless to try. She gripped the counter, listening to the raucous sound of the car's engine revving up and diminishing as Charlotte drove off. The day was full of the promise of rain, moiling clouds overhead and distant thunderclaps. Shari might have run off to the woods anyway, but she had no desire to today.

To keep herself from brooding, she decided to make brownies. Luckily, there was enough unsweetened chocolate for the cookbook recipe Zeke liked especially.

He might be willing to deliver some to Peter for her. A quake of thunder split the sky, and it got so dark outside that Shari turned on the light in the kitchen. She even switched on the radio, but beside the country-western channel that her mother listened to, all that was on was a talk show with people calling in about teenage drinking. Better to listen to the thunder. Once the brownies were in the oven, the thoughts she'd been avoiding crowded in on her. It didn't help to busy herself cleaning up her own mess and the sink full of dirty dishes from breakfast. The thoughts persisted.

However wary she had been of Charlotte's anger, Charlotte had been "Mother." Charlotte had been unfair and hurtful, but she had still been "Mother," that human security blanket every child needed. Now suddenly such distance had opened between them that Shari was seeing Charlotte as a person outside her parental role, not an especially nice person, with her flaring temper and her weasel way of lying when it suited her needs. She had more meanness in her than other adults had, more hate, and not all of it was directed at Shari either. Charlotte hated anyone who got in her way. Even Peter. She had moments of showering affection on him, but mostly she ignored him and was glad to leave him in his sister's charge so as not to be bothered with him. And Doug and Walter—Charlotte liked them well enough when they were out of the house. She gave them credit for earning money and digging out the driveway in winter and mowing the lawn in summer, but when their squabbling or horsing around bothered her, she would lash out at them too, scream at them to shut up and get out of her sight.

What Charlotte liked best was to sit talking about

how hard she had it over a cup of coffee with BeeJay. But when BeeJay went home, Charlotte would make remarks about her, about why BeeJay had been divorced three times and how she was a lot older than she admitted to being. There was no one to whom Charlotte was loyal, unless it was Zeke. The disappointments of her life were sad, and having three babies before she was twenty probably had been hard for Charlotte, but not hard enough so that Shari could excuse her mother's lack of human kindness.

Shari listened to the rush of water in the sink as she scrubbed the pot with the burned-on baked beans that had been left to soak overnight. If only the problem were simply that Charlotte hadn't wanted a child—any child. It would be hard to know she hadn't been wanted, but Shari could deal with that. What bothered her more was the feeling that it was her own fault that her mother didn't love her. Mrs. Wallace had said that Shari wasn't to blame. What a relief to believe that she wasn't the unloving creature Charlotte accused her of being.

Shari stood at the doorway watching the translucent streamers of rain making the earth into a batter as dark as the baking brownies. Rain drummed on the roof, slapped the windowpanes, and hissed in the leaves. The heavy green scent of summer competed with the odor of warm chocolate in the kitchen.

The front door slammed as Charlotte dashed into the house. Shari heard Walter and Doug's voices. Charlotte must have picked them up at their stand on her way home.

"Stack all that stuff in the carport and come in the back way with your muddy feet," Charlotte told them.

She herself walked into the kitchen. Her eyes went to the sink. "I see you decided to do something useful for a change," she said.

"I do a lot of things that are useful," Shari said. "I take care of Peter all the time."

Charlotte frowned. "What's got into you? I'm not telling you you did anything wrong. . . . Here," she said. "I went shopping at the mall after I stopped by to see Peter, and I brought you a new pair of pants. The ones you got are falling into holes. Here . . ." She rattled a thin paper bag, one of several she was holding. "See if they fit."

"Why didn't you ever tell me before that I wasn't Zeke's child?" Shari asked, taking the bag, but not looking into it as the question that had been at the back of her mind shot out of her mouth.

"You still chewing that over? All right, if you must know, I promised Zeke that I'd never tell you, and if you hadn't made me so mad—"

"Will Zeke be angry if I tell him I know?"

Charlotte slapped the packages onto the kitchen table and squared off for a fight. "You threatening me? Think I care what you tell him? Zeke'd never hold anything against me for long. He's still crazy about me, for your information, Miss Shari Ape Face."

"I wasn't threatening you, just asking," Shari said. "Because I need to talk to Zeke."

"Why?"

"To find out—" She had trouble putting her need into words. "About where I am." She looked at her mother calmly. Never before in her life had she felt as free of Charlotte. If it wasn't Shari's fault, if it was just Charlotte's nature to be mean, then Shari owed her mother nothing. No need to fear her anymore. With nothing due and nothing to expect, the bond between them was broken.

Doug and Walter tramped in the back door, dripping wet. They yanked off their muddy sneakers and dropped them on the mat beside the door.

"Boy, today was the worst!" Doug complained, heading for the towel rack. "Nobody hardly stopped by the stand. Tomorrow we're going to stay home and do something fun for a change."

"Ma, tomorrow, could you drive me by the library?" Walter asked. "I got four overdue books."

"Don't bother me now," Charlotte said as she opened the refrigerator. "Your father's going to walk in any minute, and I haven't figured out what to make for supper yet."

"Is he gonna leave again right away when he finds out Shari got home all right?" Walter asked.

"How should I know? Anyway, she's not planning to stay around for long. Wonder what he's going to say about *that* when he gets here." Charlotte gave Shari a resentful glance and smacked a pot down on the stove.

"Where are you going, Shari?" Doug asked.

"I might go to live with Mrs. Wallace," Shari said. "But I don't know for sure yet."

"What do you want to go and do that for?" Doug asked with a puzzled frown on his meaty face.

Shari shrugged. "Just because," she said. She felt Walter looking at her, all big ears and thinking eyes.

"Can one of us move into Shari's room then? Can I?" Doug asked Charlotte.

"Don't bother me about it. Ask your father."

Walter pulled a paperback out of his jeans' pocket and sat down at the kitchen table to read. Shari felt bad seeing him curl himself up into his book with nothing to say to her. He was her brother, after all. Then she remembered—no, he wasn't.

Ten

Zeke didn't get home until after Shari had gone to bed that night, but she found him sitting at the kitchen table working on his accounts the next morning. Nobody else was up yet. She was so glad to see him there and to have him to herself for once that she threw her arms around his back and hugged him uninvited. When she remembered he wasn't her real father anymore, she let go and took a step back in a sudden fit of shyness.

"What's up, Shari honey? You been having a hard time lately?" He tugged her around in front of him and kissed her, then offered her a knee to perch on. She sat on the chair across from him instead and leaned her elbows on the table.

"Zeke, is Peter getting out of the hospital soon?"

"Didn't your mother tell you? We're picking him up today."

"Oh, good! Can I go with you?"

"Sure." He sipped from his coffee mug, studying her. "Every time I come home, even if I've only been gone a day, you look more grown up and prettier."

"I'm not pretty," Shari said.

"Sure you are. Pretty as a chipmunk. You're small-boned and neat and quick."

Shari smiled. "Thanks a lot," she mocked his compliment.

"You don't think chipmunks are pretty?"

She shrugged. His broad face half covered with a stubble of on-the-road beard was so dear to her, but she made herself say, "I need to talk to you about something important, Zeke."

"I figured you might. Charlotte said she let slip about your dad."

Shari nodded, heat rising to her cheeks. It was painful to talk to the man whom she loved as a father, who wasn't her father, about the stranger who was. It didn't surprise her to hear that Charlotte had already confessed. Just the tactics she would use. Tell first so that Shari couldn't hold anything over her. Not that Shari would have, but Charlotte didn't have a high enough regard for her to know that.

"It's a pretty morning after all that rain," Zeke said. "Want to walk down the road a piece?"

"Yes." She was grateful for the offer.

"Tell you what," he said. "Why don't we go to the ravine where Peter had his accident. I ought to look that place over anyhow."

"It wasn't my fault," Shari thought to tell Zeke. "He

said he wanted to stay home, and Mother was here, so I went to see my friend, Mrs. Wallace, and then he decided to follow me."

"I know how you love him, honey. And you take good care of him too. No way did I ever think it was your fault," Zeke assured her.

Outside, a million glittering dewdrops clung to every grass blade and leaf. The air smelled of rich earth and tangy pines, better to Shari than any perfume Zeke had ever bought Charlotte. They walked together through woods so canopied with leaves that the underbrush was sparse and the ground felt springy from evergreen needles and autumns of dead oak and beech and birch and hickory leaves.

"Well, then," Zeke said when she didn't begin talking to him. "How about it? Now you know I'm not your blood father, do you still love me?"

"Me?" she asked, indignant that he could ask such a question as if she were the one to change. "I love you just as much as ever. You're who you always were. Except—"

"There is no except, Shari." He took her by the shoulders and turned her around to face him. "You're who you always were to me too. You were my little girl from the day you were born. First time you looked up at me and smiled, I loved you and I've never stopped. People ask me how many kids I've got and I say four and never think that you're any different from your brothers. Although, being a girl does make you special. Don't tell your brothers on me, but I'm partial to little girls." The grin made his face knobby and brought out the lines around his eyes, which were beaming warmly down on her.

She squeezed his hand.

"Maybe it's a good thing Charlotte told you, though I never wanted her to. I don't know," Zeke said. "She just never got over what he did to her."

"My father?"

"The man that put his seed in her and left her. *I'm* your father," Zeke said forcefully. "I'm the one raised you and don't you forget it."

"I won't. But Zeke, what was he like? You knew him, didn't you?"

"Yeah, he liked planes. Liked to show off too, always ready to take a dare. How he died was he tried to break the free-fall record and he went too long without opening his chute. When Charlotte saw in the newspaper that he'd killed himself, that was when she stopped hoping he'd come back for her and said she'd marry me. I guess I owe him something for that. Lord knows how long she would've waited if he hadn't killed himself. She sure had it bad for that fella."

"But she loves you so much—"

"Well, *now* she does. But at first I was the one did all the loving. It wasn't until after you was born that she changed. But even before she did, I considered myself a lucky fella. She was the prettiest girl in the valley and lovable, a fun-loving girl. And she had an idea about going away to New York or some big city. I guess she wanted to work for a fancy department store or something like that. The way I see it, if she hadn't fallen for that stunt man, she would've never married me. Isn't it something the way life works out, Shari?"

"Yes," she agreed. In her mind she saw him falling, a thin wiry man, exultant as the air swished by him. His body must have felt light as a bird's, as if the air were

cushioning him and he were strong enough to ride the
currents and dip and swoop and soar like a hawk, like
an eagle, free of all but the flying. He must have been
thrilled in those moments of risk and supremely happy
the day he died.

"It kind of shook me when you asked me about becoming a pilot," Zeke said. "Remember? I told you not
to say that to your mother. Now you understand why. I
never would've thought something like that could be
inherited."

"It could be accidental," she said. "Or flying might be
like a talent, like musical ability that you can inherit."

"Well, it's a mystery to me," Zeke said. "But I don't
care what you inherited from him, so long as we got it
straight who's your father."

"You are," she said happily.

"That's right." He grinned and gave her an extra
squeeze. "And mighty proud of it too."

Zeke was horrified when he saw the ledge on the far
side of the ravine. "You climbed over that by yourself?
You climbed over that and hoisted your little brother
over with you?"

Zeke was so incredulous that she said, "It's not that
hard. Watch, I'll show you." Surefooted, she ran across
the log and then from toehold to handhold, past bush
and rock until she reached the overhanging ledge. Despite his cry of alarm, she lifted herself quickly over
and stood up at the top.

"Get back down here," he said. "You're scaring the
pants off me."

"It's not as steep as it looks from the bottom," she
assured him when she had returned to his side, "and

it's the only way I can get to my friend. The road takes
too long. It's miles and miles by the road."

"You like her a lot, that lady. How come?" he asked.

"Because," Shari said and shrugged. It would insult
him to say that Mrs. Wallace was the first adult who
had ever understood her. "I guess because we both like
birds and she teaches me stuff. . . . She's nice."

"Your mother says you want to go and live with her."

"Mrs. Wallace said if I wanted to live with her, I
could."

"And you want to go?"

"Well, I'd miss you and Petey."

He squeezed her hand and said earnestly, "I'd feel
really bad if you left home before you were grown up
and ready. That's going to come soon enough." He
stroked her hair and ran his fingers down her cheek.
"Shari, you and your mother—I know a girl your age
sometimes has a hard time getting along with her own
mother."

"She hates me."

"No, she doesn't. She's a nervous woman, emotional,
you know? And she does pick on you more than on
your brothers, but she doesn't mean nothing by it." He
sounded apologetic.

"Don't worry. It's not your fault," Shari said. She
knew he couldn't help seeing Charlotte as his sweetheart, the good wife who waited at home for him to
return. He loved Charlotte blindly, but then he loved
Shari too.

They walked home through the singing woods hand
in hand. "What I'm going to do is put a climbing rope
down over that ledge so you got something to grip

going up it, a good thick rope with knots in it," Zeke said. "But don't you let Peter go up it alone."

"I won't."

"I remember when I was a kid, the places we used to climb and the things we'd try—if our parents knew the half of it, they'd of had a fit. But a kid can get hurt easy."

"I know," Shari said.

"And you know how much you and Peter mean to me. Yeah, you know now, don't you?" He hugged her.

She sat in the backseat of the car along with Walter and Doug. They dropped Walter off at the library, and Zeke and Doug went to the hardware store while Shari followed Charlotte up to Peter's room. He looked small sitting on the edge of his bed, already dressed in shorts and a tee shirt and sneakers, ready to leave.

"Shari!" he cried. They met halfway between the door and the bed and wrapped their arms tightly around each other. "Boy, did I miss you," he complained, just as she'd imagined he would. "How come you didn't come visit me?"

"Because I didn't think she should after what she did," Charlotte said when Shari didn't answer. "Listen you two, I got to go down to the cashier and fill out all kinds of papers before they let us out of here. Shari, you see to it he packs all his stuff. Zeke's going to take the six of us out to lunch on the way home."

"Wow, can I have a malted and French fries?" Peter asked.

"Maybe. We'll see," Charlotte said and disappeared.

The other bed in the room was surrounded by white

curtains on metal rods. "He's got tubes up his nose," Peter said. "He had an operation yesterday, I think." Then he whispered in Shari's ear, "I think he's going to die."

"No," Shari said. "They'll make him well, Peter. He probably just looks sick because of the operation."

"I hope so," Peter said. "I wouldn't like to die, Shari."

"No. Me either."

"I'm not going to climb on that hill alone no more."

"That's okay, Pete. I'll go with you."

"Maybe when I get bigger, then I can climb. But I'll never be as good as you."

"Sure you will."

"No, I won't. You're the best climber."

"Well, you're the best talker then."

"Oh yeah, I'm good at that. The nurses call me motor mouth. Did you miss me, Shari?"

"Very much."

"Is Blue Boy talking yet?"

"I don't know. I took him up to Mrs. Wallace's. She's keeping him for me."

"Why?"

"Just because I didn't think he'd be safe at home."

"Isn't it safe at home?"

"I think it's getting safer," she said. "Come on. Let's see what you've got to pack in here." She opened the small suitcase Charlotte had given her and began to put the few items from Peter's bedside closet into it.

The happiest days of the summer came next. "Long as I'm home again, might as well make this my vacation," Zeke had said. They went swimming at the lake twice, and one day Zeke took them to a state fair, where Peter was ecstatic because he won a large stuffed bear in a bingo game. Shari rode the tilt-a-whirl three times in a row and was fascinated by the auto thrill show in the stadium.

Shortly before school opened, she started following a body-building program that Doug had taken up and dropped, and when Peter asked her what she was doing, she said, "Getting in shape to join the air force."

"Now?"

"I have to be ready when I'm old enough."

Peter exercised with her the first day, although he couldn't do a push-up and his sit-ups were elbow-assisted. He was best at running in place. Zeke put an early end to the second exercise session by asking for help to hang a climbing rope from a tree over the lip at the top of the ravine. Peter and Shari both volunteered.

"You give Mrs. Wallace an answer to her offer yet?" Zeke asked, as they walked from the car to the tree on the back road above the ravine. He carried the coil of heavy-duty rope already knotted at intervals for easy handholds.

"Not yet," Shari said. "When your vacation is over, I'll go see her then."

"And what are you going to tell her?"

"I don't know."

"It sure would be nice if you'd make up your mind. I bet Mrs. Wallace is wondering too, Shari."

Shari looked at him in surprise. "Why should she be?"

"Well, likely she's lonely and hoping to get your company."

"I don't think so," Shari said. "That's not why she offered me a home. She doesn't mind being alone. I don't either."

He ruffled her hair, smiling. "You're such a funny kid," he said. "Half the time I can't begin to figure what you got in your head. I'll tell you the truth. I'm going to feel real bad if you're not home to greet me next time I get off the road."

"Me too," Peter said.

"I won't go unless I have to," was all Shari could tell them.

Charlotte had been easy to get along with while Zeke was home, but even after he left, she kept her black moods to herself and treated Shari with a cautious respect. One morning Shari was doing her exercises in the middle of the living room while Peter kept count for her rather than do the exercises himself.

"What are you doing, training for the Olympics?" Charlotte asked.

"No, just making myself stronger," Shari said.

"What for?"

"So if I want to join the air force some day."

"You really think ahead, don't you?" Charlotte said, and then grudgingly, "I wish I had when I was a kid."

"You could do something now," Shari said. "You could get a job or something. I'd watch Peter for you after school."

Charlotte tapped her unlit cigarette against the pack from which she'd just removed it. "I thought you were leaving us."

"If you need me, I could stay. Mrs. Wallace wants me

to help her with the bird banding, but I could take Peter with me sometimes for that. It'd work out."

"How come you're so eager for me to get a job?" Charlotte asked.

"I think you'd like being out of the house more."

"Zeke wouldn't like it though if I was."

"He would if he thought it was making you happier."

"I'll think about it," Charlotte said. She started out of the room, stopped and turned around to add, "I forgot to tell you, Mrs. Wallace called and asked how you and Peter are doing."

"I'm going to visit her soon, today maybe."

"What do you want to be friends with an old party like that for anyway?"

"I like her."

"Yeah? I wonder. I wonder if she just don't feel sorry for you because you told her I beat you up and treat you mean."

"I never told her anything like that."

"You didn't? Then how come she offered to let you come and live with her?"

"Because—" Shari stopped exercising, trying to remember how it had been. Had she betrayed Charlotte to Mrs. Wallace? Shari thought guiltily that possibly she had. "I don't usually talk about you to anybody. I was just feeling bad that time because Petey was in the hospital, and you said it was my fault, and I was afraid you'd do something to the bird like you did to Chirpy last summer."

Charlotte gasped. "I never did nothing to your parakeet."

"You opened the window and let him fly out. I saw you."

Charlotte was silent. Her face turned red and she looked as if she were about to cry. "You're always making me feel bad," she accused. "Right from the start you raised your arms to Zeke and ran away from me. Soon as you could walk, you ran away from me, and you never wanted to cuddle the way the boys did when they were little. Sure, I get mad sometimes, but it's your own fault. You're the one."

"I can't help being the way I am, Ma," Shari said quietly.

"Yes, you can," Charlotte said. "If I can, you can too." She stood there and wiped away an overflow of tears with the back of her hand. Then she looked at Shari, who was watching her, trying to understand why Charlotte was crying. "You can take your bird back," Charlotte said. "I'm not about to do anything to harm it."

After lunch, Shari retrieved the crystal bird from its nesting place in her boot, wrapped it in a bandanna and tied it to the loop of her jeans. She told Peter she was going to visit Mrs. Wallace, and he asked to come along.

Charlotte was on the phone talking excitedly to Bee-Jay when Shari interrupted her to tell her where she and Peter were going. The hand with the cigarette tucked between the fingers waved her on.

"Like I say," Charlotte told BeeJay, "I could come in part time whenever you need me and handle the appointment book and the cash register, and— Sure, why not?"

August heat lay heavily on them as they walked. It

felt good to get into the shade of the dense woods. "When are we going to pan for gold again?" Peter asked.

"Tomorrow if you want," she said. The idea didn't attract her especially, but there were so few summer days left before school began. Then, she knew, Peter would be absorbed by the lively activities of his own age group and not so dependent on her for company.

When she returned to school, she planned to go to the library and read up on the air force and find out just how to go about making a career in the service. That her father had been a pilot was an omen. Even though he'd never really been her father, he'd left her a direction in the seed that was all he'd given of himself to Charlotte.

It would be good if Charlotte got a job and got out of the house more. It would be better for Shari if Charlotte got a job. She'd be less bored, and she had promised about Blue Boy. Shari was still mulling it over when she saw Mrs. Wallace standing on the bridge that spanned her pond, throwing out bread crumbs.

"Well, what a nice surprise to see you two," she called to them.

"What are you doing?" Peter asked.

"Feeding the fish. Look." She pointed to moving crescents that looked like chips of orange sunset in the water.

"Wow!" Peter said. "You got a lot of fish. Can I feed some?"

She handed him the plastic bag she was holding. "Be my guest," she said and turned to Shari. "Looks as if your little brother is recovered. How are you doing?"

"Fine," Shari said. "I came to make a trade with you, your crystal bird for Blue Boy."

"Oh, you want him back, do you? Think he's safe enough now?"

"I think so. Things are getting better. . . . I want to thank you for what you offered. You know, about me living with you? But I've decided to stay home with Zeke and Peter—and my mother."

"You and your mother doing better together?"

"I hope so. Maybe," Shari said.

"Good. That's very good news, and remember, I'll be here if you should need me anytime."

"Oh, you'll be seeing a lot of me because of the bird banding," Shari said and added, "Also because you're my best friend, Mrs. Wallace."

Mrs. Wallace laughed and said, "That's an honor. I don't have too many friends I admire more than you, Shari."

The compliment embarrassed Shari, but it pleased her too. With Peter trailing behind, she followed Mrs. Wallace into the house to the big picture window in the living room where Blue Boy's cage hung. The parakeet hopped immediately onto the finger Shari extended to him. Then he ducked his head and blinked his eyes and chuckled at her rapidly as if he had a lot to tell her.

"I'm going to concentrate on teaching him to talk," Shari said. "I bet he'll learn fast."

"He's certainly a sociable fellow." Mrs. Wallace's face crinkled with amusement as she spoke.

"He likes to be with people just like Peter and my mother do," Shari said.

"Some creatures don't know how to enjoy their own company the way you and I do," Mrs. Wallace said.

"I enjoy a lot of things in life," Shari said. "I guess I'm pretty lucky."

"Are you?" Mrs. Wallace asked softly. "Well, perhaps you are. You've got the strength to fly free in the world, and it's a kind of luck to have that."

"Yes," Shari agreed. She stroked the blue-feathered head delicately with one finger, glad that her friend understood. Then she smiled as it came to her suddenly what it meant to be strong. She was free. Her fears could no longer cage her. One day, like the hawk, she would spread her wings and soar.